ANGELS IN MY LIFE

Robert Mason

ANGELS IN MY LIFE - POETRY

*A Poet who sees and talks
with the Angels*

My name is Robert Mason, and I can see and communicate with Angels, especially our Guardian Angels. I am able to feel them with me every day.

My poetry expresses some of the messages that I receive from the Angels in Heaven. The unconditional love and beauty of Heaven and the Angels impacts me constantly because I experience them every day.

There are many different types of Angelic beings in the dimension of Heaven. We can describe many of them as Angels, and Guardian Angels.

My own proof of Heaven was through a spiritual experience of an Archangel that changed my life forever. It is best expressed in the following poem that I wrote shortly after.

The Archangel

The first of May, ninenteen ninety-nine
an Archangel appeared before me, Divine,
Spring morning, sun shining,
air sweet as wine,

the beauty and radiance before me a sign
from Heaven

I bowed down in fear, but fear did not last
Archangel before me, from Holy Scriptures past,
His flowing robes, radiant, shone so bright as I saw,
A face of understanding, a moment beyond awe.
I was drawn to His eyes, full of love I was seeing,
He knew who I was, knew my life, knew my being
Unconditional love, and forgiveness for mistakes I was feeling

"Come with me" was the message, and I swiftly did rise
A path of light from Heaven, then to my surprise,
Into view came a place of landscape, beauty, so real
Green valleys, trees, flowers, vivid colours, I could feel
The air that I breathed was unconditional love,
All around me, surrounding, and a sense
of Higher Heavens above.

"This is "First Heaven", Archangel did say,
"A place of rest for souls when they leave life's day"
I could see people in joy, as they danced in this place,
Where all good souls enter from our human race
There were houses and gardens, and white buildings too
A library in Heaven holding a book of life for you.

Archangel, radiant, up again we did rise
To a Higher Heaven of cloud, and to my surprise,
Angels were working, sending healing for life
Helping humanity through problems and strife.

The Angels nearby turned towards me and smiled,
They bowed down to Archangel, and I stopped for a while
Above me a Light of Third Heaven of our Creator
The Source of all Purpose, God of Love, and our Saviour
.....Jesus Christ with the Father

"It is time to return," Archangel did say
"I have a purpose for you, to help others each day"
"The Angels will bring visions and messages to you,
For those in grief from bereavement, so
you can help them through"
"Another gift will be healing, though your body be weak,
The Angels will bring healing, for those
who seek...Healing from you"
"A gift of seeing the First Heaven, whenever you need
A gift of knowledge of Life's meaning
The Universe, the Seed...Of Life"

I suddenly was back, my feet on the ground,
Archangel was gone, no-one near but the sound
Of a perfect Spring morning,
Birds singing around
...With the joy of Life

The spiritual experience showed me that Heaven is a very real and beautiful place.

My work with the Angels is often to help ease the pain of grief when someone we love passes. We may never get over grief, but we can get through it, and move forward in our lives again...

Now you're Gone

You were here yesterday,
And now you're gone, passed away,
Cruel death has victory

News came swift that you had died,
It couldn't be, I screamed, denied,

Grief took hold, I cried and cried.

There are no answers from the world around
If you'd been religious would salvation
be found?

This busy world knows not what to say,
Like an express train on their way,
Material lives, living for today.

Science claims the answers in this modern world,
Life is dust to dust, so live to the full,
Young or old, boy or girl.

My grief takes hold and overwhelming,
Bewildered, lost, darkness closing in
Can't accept won't see you again.

My eyes are blind, but you can see,
I just don't feel you near to me.
Your soul is near, you still exist,
Life's cruel illusion is a mist

Your soul is free of all the pain,
Yet you're surprised, you are the same.
Heaven is beautiful, you know that now,
Others you loved are there somehow

Heaven is real, green valleys and trees,
Flowers caressed by gentle breeze,
Colours vivid, no pain, no fear,
A place like home made ready
for you there.

You try to reach to tell me this,
Yet the wall between us, impenetrable mist

of material world teaching,
Souls don't exist
Leaves me trapped in grief,
Time stops, I twist
...and cry.

The Angels encourage us to stop in our busy life and feel the spiritual realities of beauty and peace...

In Stillness

In stillness, look at a beautiful flower,
A bloom of colour, and fragrance,
Nature's finest hour

In stillness, gaze at night-time sky,
The stars, the universe,
And wonder why.

In stillness, let spirit wander free,
Sense the love of God,
True reality.

In stillness, and peace,
Inwardly pray,
For strength and guidance
On life's difficult way.

In stillness you may find
That time matters not,

Timeless peace rediscovered
Perhaps almost forgot

The Angels tell me that Heaven knows some of our future

Seeing The Future

What If...
The big things in our future are determined in our past,
Free Will just takes care of our everyday tasks.

We have no memory of past existense
that made us whom we are,
Yet, deep-down feelings inside somehow seem to draw...
Our lives in a certain direction every time
Life can be good, can be hard, not always fine.

Our Guardian Angels know our Life Plan,
Whom we'll be, whom we'll meet,
The places we will live, every town, every street

If we live a bad life, our Guardian Angels won't be near,
We feel uncertain of the future, lives over-shadowed by fear,
If we stray from our Life Plan, make mistakes, go astray,
This is shown to us in Life Review, at the end of Life's Day

Try to be closer to our Guardian Angels,
We can do this by gaining empathy
for people, for nature... feel love and humility
Our Guardian Angel now with us,
unconditional love will set us free.

Intuitive visions of our future,
Two paths ahead will come to see,
We can change a path of pain
to a path of joy...true destiny

Mind thoughts are racing, if only we truly knew
This poem still holds a secret,
"What Ifs" can really be true.

The Angels teach me to look at the world from a different perspective to help my understanding of the meaning of life.

Our limited senses

Our physical senses are limited, and few,
There are things we can discover
If the truth we knew
We cannot see, touch, hear, smell or taste gravity
Yet, we can feel it,
Perhaps the strongest force in the universe
Science teaches, we believe it

We cannot see, touch, hear, smell or taste radio and
Television signals,
Around us, everywhere today,
carrying messages and entertainment they bring us.

We cannot see, touch, hear, smell or taste our soul,
Science denies our soul exists

Yet, our soul energy manifests in all
human expression, emotion,
and activity
This most important evidence science has missed

Oneness of Soul

Our soul energy is a conscious energy
It is all of whom we are within
Deep inside it is the "I" or "Me"
We may feel like the only "One"
We are all connected to a spiritual Oneness
In Heaven of the Spiritual dimension
Our true, familiar home,
Of conscious energy, love and creation.

Unity of Soul

If we cause hurt or harm to someone,
Or to any living thing that has a soul
We are hurting a part of the Oneness,
of which together we are whole
As some might say "Hurting a part of
ourselves, Scoring an own goal".

Guardian Angels

Who or what are Guardian Angels?
They are as people
Who have lived through many lives?
Are spiritually grown, now sufficiently wise
To guide us through our lives

Their soul energy is pure and wonderful,
Radiant as the sun
Spiritual beings so beautiful
They bring the unconditional love of Heaven
They know our inner being,
Our mistakes, our good and bad, our feelings
Forgiveness isn't needed
For their compassion and understanding is absolute

The Angels teach me that the most important spiritual quality is to be caring to others, to animals and nature.

A Person Who Cares

"Please find me food, I'm hungry,
Please give me water I'm dry,
Don't leave me, don't ignore me,
Or I will surely die"
"You are a stranger here amongst us
In this war-torn famine land
Please show me that you care,
Show me you understand"

The stranger stopped and said, "Your suffering I understand"
"I will lead you away from here,
Come, please take my hand,
To a place of food abundant

Where water freely flows
To a land of peace and freedom
Where children learn and grow"

The suffering all followed this stranger
Her goodness they all knew
Are you a caring person?
Could this stranger, perhaps, be you?

I am shown by the Angels that in Heaven everyone is equally important, no matter what our position was in life.

Just a Number

To the world I'm just a number,
Along with all the rest,
Never getting anywhere or earning much,
Although I always keep trying my best
I know I'll never be famous,
And wealth never comes my way,
What little I earn goes on food and home,
As I struggle through each day.
So, what colour is there in my life?
I ask myself many times
The same work and routines every day
Are the usual experience of mine.
Yet what of the rich and famous
With their houses and property Fine?
For a person can only make use of
One room and one chair at a time
We are all breathing same air as each other
And however our friendships are sought
The best and truest of friends
Can never, ever be bought.

A scenic view and the beauty of nature
Are things that we all can see,
And the experience of sport, art and music
Can cost little, and often found free.
So when I think of myself as a number,
It's only an emotional test
The truth is we all are important
Yes, you and I are as good as the Best!

I have given many thousands of people Angel messages concerning a soul of a loved one, now in Heaven. On every occasion the Angels show me that souls in Heaven have their memories and the same character.

Memories

Days of old, days of gold,
My memories are as autumn shades.
Life was "Nothing special" at the time
But looking back I can now define
Those special moments that stand out
With a warmth and fondness that removes all doubt
That the "Nothing special" was important to me
In this life that to others seems so ordinary.

Angels work constantly to support nature.

The most important spiritual quality is to be loving and caring towards others, towards, animals, and nature and the environment. It is a measure of our spiritual growth.

Daffodil

Oh daffodil, your beauty of moment
Last forever, if time never spent.

All year you hide away from sight,
To appear in gardens as Springtime Light

Yellow radiance as the sun,
In coat of green your leaves are spun

Soft breeze caress, you move and dance
Flower of love, colour of romance

You are Spring, and Spring is you
You are my image of life renew

My spirit lifts with you nearby,
I scarce can turn away my eye

Oh daffodil, your beauty of moment
And eternal dreams forever dreamt

Having been an active Christian for most of my life until aged mid-fifties, I left my Church so that I could fully accept my gift of seeing Angels. Since then, I have helped many thousands of people in a way that is hard to find elsewhere. I know that the unconditional love of God is with me through the Guardian Angels that help me in this work...........

Life On Hold

I was greeted at the door, I felt welcomed, and walked in,
A family needing help, booked for Angel messages reading
"Our family want to hear whatever you can say,
But first please meet my Mum,
Just follow me this way"
In the middle of the home, a room... bed, table, flowers,
Two armchairs, and tv to while away the hours,
Of a lady age late sixties, nicely dressed, on her own,
Living with her family, yet somehow quite alone

"I see your husband in spirit", I couldn't help but say
"A man who truly loved you, and still loves from far, away"

The lady smiled, then her eyes dropped,
"Can I continue?" words I said
She whispered "Yes" and I revealed,
My vision, a hospital bed,
Her husband pale, on life support, a doctor stood nearby,
I told this lady my vision,
She began to cry,
"I killed him, I took his life, for six years I've hid away,
I haven't left this room,
I stopped my life that day"

Shocked by her painful outburst, then
my vision came more clear
The doctor asking permission, "No hope for him my dear",
To switch off life support....the lady froze with fear

I was looking at the scene, as if a birds –eye view,
She left the ward just walking, not knowing what to do

The scene played out in front of me, shortly she returned
The doctor turned to see, inside her feelings burned,
In spirit her husband came, his lifeless body set him free
He whispered in her ear:
"Please say "Yes" and release me"
And "Yes" is what she said, not knowing how she could,
She blamed herself for saying yes, and didn't want to live

I described to her my vision, "Oh my.... you couldn't know this
I believe you, and now I see ...my husband wanted this"
"I know now I didn't kill him, no longer carry blame"
I said "Your husband wants to see you... live your life again"

I left her to give more readings, then at the evening's end
I went into the lounge, and was greeted like a friend
"Mum's life is no longer on hold, tomorrow
she wants to go shopping
New life, new strength, Mum's back, after
years of praying and hoping!"

Who or What are Angels?

Heaven is another dimension. This isn't anything to fear because it is our true home. Our soul energy is made of the same energies as Heaven. Our life in the physical form as human beings has always been nothing more than a temporary home with joy and love contrasted by times of unhappiness and fear.
I don't always see Angels having wings. I perceive that visions of Angels in modern or ancient times would be in their true radiance. They radiate spiritual energies that appear as light.

The visual effect of radiating light is easily understood. Spiritual energies that are breaking through from another dimension are not affected by gravity. An Angelic Being appearing as a vision will most likely appear somehow suspended in the air. To ancient people, the only way that any living thing could appear in the air is if, like a bird, they had wings to fly. Hence. Angels with their beautiful, radiating, shimmering light were described by witnesses as having wings so they could fly.

I cannot emphasise enough how Heaven views all souls as being equal. There are Archangels as my very real spiritual experience describes. Archangels are closer to the purpose of the Source of whom religions may name "God".

Beyond the Archangels there are Wise Beings who have the authority to judge our soul's progress in our recent life. I am not able to say how they judge, but it would seem that spiritual progress is acquired by being genuinely loving and caring in actions towards other people, and towards animals, nature and the environment. Spiritual regression is when a soul has caused hurt to others and nature. All people in life make many mistakes and we are forgiven for times when we caused hurt. It helps heal the situation if we genuinely feel aware of the hurt that we caused and are aware of our wrongdoings.

Our Angel companions are with us much of the time. We are viewed with respect and loved unconditionally. Life is a gift for our soul to have adventure and experience and importantly, learn. It is deliberate that we can't see Angels or hear them speak to us.

The Angels from Heaven work in unconditional love and only ever bring positive, helpful messages. They communicate through our feelings, our intuition and our conscience. We will never, or rarely hear a voice in our mind. We can learn how to recognise the messages from the Angels and I describe how this works in the following narrative "Aspects of the Soul"

ASPECTS OF THE SOUL

I see all human souls as an energy that is just "One". Within the "One" we actually create our own areas in which our soul may resonate. I call these areas "Aspects of the Soul". They vary from person to person, and can be many areas, but I broadly categorise them into the Aspects of Higher Self, Middle Self, and Lower Self.

Aspects Of The Soul-Middle Self

Like an unseen wind that blows to who knows where
Our invisible soul energy, is whom we are, always there
As a gentle breeze on a fine summer day
Our soul may be gentle and full of play
Storms come in our lives and our souls energise
As destructive winds in a storm, are our actions ever wise?

Our souls have three aspects, Higher, Middle, Low
In which our soul resonates, in these poems I will show.
Most of life's time our soul resonates in self-centre,
The middle level of our existence we most often enter

Self-centred is normal for food, shelter, money,
Entertainment, life journeys, stressful or funny

Materialistic world adverts target us every day
To buy more desires, phone, car, holiday,
Shop for leisure, shop for pleasure,
Spend, spend every day,
In Middle Self we are grounded,
our very being might go astray,
We may not feel our Guardian Angels,
Many in this world lose their way.

Aspects Of The Soul - Lower Self

Many souls resonate at times in lower self,
Primitive, worse than animal, greed, seeking power,
and wealth.

They never put their thoughts in other people's place,
Cold hearts destroy lives, a scourge on the human race

Psychological bullies, cause physical hurt, pain and fear
Steal energies from those around, family,
friends, and others near,

Living each day in Lower Self, Guardian
Angels cannot get through,
To live like that is a free will choice
Negative energy may take over you
And leave you devoid of love, hurting others on the way
Precious lives destroyed
by self-centred people every day.

Aspects Of The Soul - Higher Self

A caring, loving soul may lift-up to Higher Self,
Needs of others before themselves, not concerned with
Wealth
They have a secret, I will share, for tired they often may be
When helping others they feel stronger
Their soul feels more energy
…………From the Angels

In Higher Self, unconditional love,
Is a perfect energy

Our Angels connect more closely, setting our soul free,
..............Of Life's burden's

Our Life Plan will be clearer,
For our Angels already know,
They hold a vision of our future
Whom we'll meet, and where we'll go

Guardian Angels speak through our feelings,
Intuitive knowing of what's wrong and right,
Ways forward through our problems
Our life now filled with Light

In Middle Self, and Lower self, our Angels are still there
We may not know their presence,
Until we resonate in love, and care
.........for others

Become more loving, and more caring,
Qualities of spiritual strength, and grace,
Let us learn, let us grow,
We can make the world a better place

The wonderful, amazing and profound impact on our lives of becoming closer to our Guardian Angels and discovering the Angels that are there to help each one of us can be life changing!

A "CALLING"

Ever wondered why some people are so determined to do something to help others? Why some people are determined to work helping animals, nature, or the environment?

I believe that many people are given a "Calling". This is a gift from Heaven to do a particular task. The task is part of a Divine Plan to make sure that every aspect of life has people interested in caring and working to cherish, protect, repair and bring healing
Our Guardian Angels know this Divine Plan and work to help those with a Calling to help them fulfil their inner driving force to care for other people, or care for animals, nature, and planet Earth.

A Calling

Someone called my name, no-one there
I heard it again – from where?
Perhaps imamgination, yet, inner-feelings, new sensation
Heightened awareness, inspiration.
I must help others, I must show care,
New ideas in my mind, guiding me – where?
Yes, I now see it clearly, people suffering out there.

I know it won't be a perfect way,
Somehow, I'll help others each day,
No longer thinking just about me,
Money, pleasure, living selfishly.

A new driving force, like fire within,
I must get started, I must begin,
Trying to help others, new goals in sight,
It matters more that I try,
Than to always get it right.

Touching lives, kindness, goodness, share,
Giving, helping,
My new purpose is to care.

Do we spend time earning money, polluting the planet, or do we focus our efforts on climate change prevention?

Money

When I think about money,
Food, clothing, home costs, are a problem sometimes,
And I need a little money for extra things
The interests and pleasures of mine.

I often wish I had more money
my income a bigger share,
I could buy things I've always wanted, travel anywhere.

Yet, when I think of what I care for most, remind myself I try,
True friends, family, the beauty of nature,
Money just can't buy.

Animals and Birds have a soul energy, not as big as a human soul, but still loved by God.

Little Bird

Little bird, on a tree branch up there,
Singing your song across the air,
A message to other birds, I am sure,
To me your song is pleasant and pure.
Little bird always seeking food to eat,
Then flying away to your safe retreat,
Little bird, you know how to make your nest,
Raise your young, and look your best
Little bird, little bird, on a tree branch, up there,
Singing your song across the air
You know love, you have a soul
I know you're aware...

Poems about Planet Earth

The River

Life, where are you going?
Life, where are you going? as river, onward flowing,
Twisting left, meandering right, different
ways, new paths in sight
New things to do, feelings renew.

When the river flows calm and wide,
All seems well on life's journey ride,
River moves faster, playful dance,
Tumbling over rocks, scattered by chance,
Life moves faster, heart beats faster too,
We're high then low, happy, then blue.

Then, dance is echoed by thunder sound
Inside apprehension, roar all around,
River tumbles down rapid falls,
No more calm, rage crashing calls.
Life's storms will also come our way,
No matter sun or rainy day,
We're torn in half, emotional pain,
No calm, no harmony again?

Then, still and clear, fresh waters reach
In life new light, new hope, beseech.
Life, where are you going, full circle again?
Or some new twist in your hidden game?
As river meanders to distant sea,
Life's good times, and bad, steer my destiny,
With my love for nature, and our planet Earth
Guiding me.

Walking

A gentle Spring morning, the sun and blue sky,
delicate white clouds, floating high,
I walked up a steep path, into the trees,
Tall branches filtered sun, calm shelter from breeze.

A timeless rustling of leaves, restless movements of air,
As the wind high above rushed to who knows where,
Wildflowers of blue, lilac, yellow around,
Birds singing above me, their own sweet sound.

I felt at peace with the world, aware of creation,
A beautiful, warm, uplifting sensation.

I wandered endlessly on, not once did I tire,
'Till end of day came, the sky alive with fire,
The red, orange and purple, its beauty show,
Sunset o'er distant mountains, melted into a glow.

I prayed inwardly for our world, and felt heightened awareness,
My soul in harmony with creation,
Through nature's sweet caress.

Derwent Water, Cumbria

Enchanted places on Earth
have many portals to Heaven,
Derwentwater, Cumbria is a place of them

I walked an easy path, through trees on Friar's Cragg
My spirit now uplifted, my weary feet didn't drag
Then, before my eyes unfolded the lake
and Borrowdale
Morning mist and distant mountains

rose-up to tell a tale,
Of majesty and wonder that many authors inspire
Poetic feelings intense, awakened, hearts that burnt on fire
To rest in this place forever, so many would desire

I spoke with my Guardian Angel, felt harmony inside
With all of life in nature
Joy I could not hide

A portal travels both ways, for those in Heaven
can still see,
This precious view that they experienced
when they were alive and free.

I see them with my clairvoyant gift
I hear the words that they once wrote
This place enchanted, I see more Angels
The moment forever caught
In my soul, my very being
That will live through eternity
I will return someday in spirit,
Heaven on Earth is where I'll be.

Grasmere Cumbria

Serene, beautiful, calm, majestic
Inspirational, classical, peaceful, poetic
All these feelings as I walked your path side
A mere not a lake, your calm water's wide
Deer Bolts Wood I roam, evening creeps up on me
Darkness comes quickly, I cared not, I was free
Of city life, suburban jungle, not really me.

Warm caress of summer evening, sky melted to a glow
Of fiery red between high mountains, natures beauty show
I wander now towards the village, warm hotel to be my host

Then I saw a light before me, my mind
perplexed, was this a ghost?
A light of white and strange in darkness,
moving yet there was no breeze,
Floating above, across the mere, meandering back into the trees,
Was this the soul of classical poet whose heart belonged to this
fine place?
Still dwells amongst this place of magic, where
early Springtime daffodils grace?

I felt no fear as light approached me, I
was a stranger in fairy land.
I had to know, I had to ask, who are you? my need to understand,
Then a whispering voice around me,
from the water and the land
"I am no ghost of classical poet, he was
my friend, he knew me well
I am an Angel, to care for nature, the woods,
the animals, 'tis here I dwell"

"This is a place of Angels, love and healing through eternity,
This evening, now, a special moment, all of life in harmony,
Remember this for all your years, know how precious life can be,
Please try to work to save our planet, for
poets of old, for you and me."
Angels are working to help avert the worst
consequences of Climate Change.

Death of Nature

From trees and plants that lived and died,
through millions of years,

My treasure hidden underground, away
from human wars and tears,
I am fossil fuels, long dormant,
I have been waiting for this time
Of resurrection by humanity
On their evolution climb.

Stored from death of nature long ago,
Forests died, forming coal, oil below.

Captured sun that shone on Jurassic lands,
Now making fire at people's command
To power industry, cars, boats and planes
Human beings unaware of my end game
From death of forests and life, during eras long ago,
Destruction to nature, my flames now released, in one go.

My fire, my energy abused,
Coal, oil, and gas, overused,
I bring climate change, pollution,
Death to nature, pain, confusion.

Plastics in oceans, polluted cities, toxic air,
Can nature recover? Fossil fuels don't care.

ANGELS IN MY LIFE - THE BOOK

Anne had helped her mother nurse her grandfather George, her mother's father, through a long period of illness. In his final weeks of life, he had been in hospital but had requested to be transferred home to spend his last days with his remaining family. The family home, as with many modern homes, has a voice activated internet search unit in the lounge.

Two days after her George's death, Anne came home from shopping, accompanied with her mother. The internet search unit had activated "Play music" which was sounding out loud as they entered their home. No-one else was in the building. The song it was playing was Grandfather George's favourite song. They were both bewildered and surprised and had no logical answers for why the music should be playing. The music was loud, and Anne's mother exclaimed, away from the voice activated unit in the kitchen: "This is too loud". To their further amazement the song immediately quietened.

Anne's sister, who lived elsewhere, phoned minutes later to say that music was playing in her home without her instruction. She was quite shocked by this and further amazed that the song the internet playing was the one chosen to play at the funeral service. "Could it be Grandfather George?" was the question the family asked themselves. "How could George be so clever as to manipulate a voice activated internet search device? He had suffered mild dementia prior to his death."

As a clairvoyant I later heard this account from Anne. I asked the Angels concerning this incident and received immediate confirmation that the music playing in both households had been a sign from George that his soul had survived death. We are fully restored with our memories once we reach Heaven in our state as a soul. However, we are not clever enough to operate computer search engine devices in our soul state, but those in Heaven are. Heaven is the source of infinite intelligence, of all knowledge, and our Guardian Angels find it easy to help us because they access this knowledge.

I have heard many accounts of signs being witnessed by people grieving the loss of loved ones who have passed. One lady described a butterfly flying around the church where the funeral of her father was being held. The time of year was mid-winter. I am confident that all of these signs are at the wishes of the deceased person, but actually made to happen by the Angels, Angels are everywhere trying to help us all through life. yet many people are unaware of this.

Who and What are Angels?

I see Angels of different order who have different purposes. Archangels may appear with the specific purposes of bringing messages to help in times of human crisis.

Higher Angels may appear with a radiance that might be seen as wings. I have witnessed these many times, especially at religious sites. I can only communicate briefly with such Angels, and I usually ask why they are there.

Some Angels work in nature, helping to heal and maintain the continuity of life in insects, animals, birds, plants, flowers and trees. They are also at work maintaing life in the oceans. Although I often see these Angels they are busy helping nature so I know they won't divert their attention to me for more than a minute.

The Angels that work directly with human beings are Guardian Angels. I often call these "Angel Guides" because we each have at least one such Angel accompanying us through life, and their most important work is in trying to guide us. I see Guardian Angels with many people when I observe them spiritually. They assume a male or female appearance, and display a radiance of colours of the rainbow.

Another important type of Angel is a healing Angel, I see these shimmering with colours specific to the healing energies that they channel. Our Guardian Angels often organise the attendance of Healing Angels because they truly know when spiritual healing is needed.

Guardian Angels are the ones that are closest to us. All spiritual beings in Heaven are equal. There is no ranking of importance. Some Angels are Higher Ascended in terms of spiritual growth. Guardian Angels are not as highly ascended, but still have access to the "Oneness" of all knowledge and wisdom in Heaven. Guardian Angels are often helped by the higher spiritual beings in times of human suffering.

Angels work closely with those on Earth, and with animals and nature, and they often specialise. Some are dedicated to Guiding us. Some are dedicated to Healing.

Heaven is Real

Heaven is real. Angels are real. They are the link between Heaven and ourselves living as human beings on Earth. Angels bring healing to ourselves and to animals and all of life in nature. A special kind of Angel, Guardian Angels, accompany us through life to try to guide us. However, many, many people don't believe in Guardian Angels because they have no evidence that they exist. Do you want to sense Angels? The best way to gain the spiritual abilities to sense Angels is to learn a special type of clairvoyance. This involves learning to see the universe around us differently.

We often think of clairvoyants as having a natural, mysterious spiritual gift. As a spiritual researcher I have discovered that acquiring the spiritual abilities of clairvoyance can be learnt to some degree by many people, although perhaps not everyone. My name is Robert Mason and through over forty years of spiritual research I discovered how to be clairvoyant. My abilities are equal to the best psychic mediums even though I wasn't clairvoyant when I was younger. A special type of clairvoyant ability has helped me see Angels and sense their communications. I have discovered how to open up my spiritual senses and perceive the visions, messages and healing from Heaven and the Angels.

Why should we learn to sense Angels?

- When we open ourselves up to sensing Angels we may lose fear of our mortality
- We can acquire the spiritual gift of sensing our Guardian Angels and listen as they try to guide ourselves and others with answers concerning problems and worries in life.
- We can be helped by the Angels to see visions and receive messages from loved ones who have passed across to Heaven. Working with Angels we may temporarily reunite those whom we are helping through a mediumship reading with the souls of loved ones in Heaven.
- With the help of Angels we might clairvoyantly sense our own

loved ones whose souls are in Heaven.
- We can sense Angels guiding us and receive their messages, healing and visions
- The Angels may give us premonitons of the future, together with guidance to help avoid bad situations
- The Angels sometimes help us see through to Heaven

These are wonderful gifts that can help transform our lives and those around us that we choose to help. Life can become safer, happier and fulfilling.

Perhaps most important of all in the challenging times of the twenty-first century:
The Angels from Heaven are trying to work through individual people to guide us in our lives to work to prevent further climate change and damage to the biodiversity of nature and the environment. Acquiring a heightened spiritual awareness helps us sense the messages that our Guardian Angels bring us, and to be guided by Heaven and help save our precious plant Earth.

CHAPTER ONE

Learning to sense Heaven

This book is an introduction into learning about Angels and a special kind of clairvoyance that can be acquired through study in order to sense Angels. I describe how Angels are essential in helping us receive spiritual messages and healing from Heaven. Much of the book contains references to our Guardian Angels. We all have one or more Guardian Angels who communicate with us. We can learn to recognise the many ways in which Angels try to help us. We may begin to sense the Angels as we become spiritually aware through the study of this special clairvoyance. The world will become a better place if many more people can acquire the gift a heightened spiritual perception and be guided by our Guardian Angels from Heaven in the difficult years of the Twenty-first century that lay ahead. The revelations in this book are intended to be a foundation in the knowledge needed to become spiritually aware of Angels. We may, with an open mind, gradually acquire the skills to sense messages from them and also experience the healing that they bring in real, tangible and miraculous ways.

At the time of writing I am age in my seventies, and still working in my career as an accountant. I have lived a normal family life with all the challenges that life gives us. In my spare time I have been a spiritual researcher for over forty years. My spiritual research led me to discovering the ability to be clairvoyant, and I have helped many thousands of people with my gift. My abilities gained through research have helped me become a locally acclaimed clairvoyant, psychic and medium. I have always recognised that it is the Angels from Heaven, especially my Guardian Angel, that brings me the messages and healing to help others.

I WANT TO TEACH AS MANY PEOPLE AS POSSIBLE A SPECIAL CLAIRVOYANCE THAT ALLOWS US TO SENSE ANGELS

What are the benefits of learning to sense Heaven and the Angels?

1) The first benefit is to lose our fear of mortality. We will learn to sense Angels, and perhaps at times see through to Heaven. We can recognise Angel messages, and even experience signs and visions from loved ones who are in Heaven.

2) Our Guardian Angels try to guide us towards a safe, happy, and fulfilling life. We can live with greater confidence, and less of the cold inner feelings that stress and worry bring into our lives,

3) We can in certain ways work with the Angels to be a channel for Angel healing to people.

4) We can even learn to receive premonitions of the future. If we are tuned-in to Heaven through the heightening of our spiritual senses, we can be guided by Heaven to make our own positive efforts to work in helping the world around with the huge global concerns brought about by pandemics and climate change.

I teach spiritual knowledge to those who were not previously able to believe in the reality or sincerity of claivoyant abilities. A naturally gifted clairvoyant and psychic will usually be a person who is more open than most people to sensing spiritual energies. Some may experience problems because they are open to all spiritual energies, including negative energy and must learn to control how these energies influence them. An important part of my teaching is to show how learn to discern between what we sense from the Angels and Heaven, and what are best described as "Negative energies" that are also all around us on the Earth plain, Messages from Angels can be picked up by learning to open ourselves to the positive energies from Heaven. I call this special type of clairvoyance "Tuning-In to Heaven". The energies from Heaven are always sensed with the unconditional love that Heaven feels for us. Alongside this we need to learn to recognise negative energies and how to block such energies so they can't influence us.

What form do messages from the Angels take? When a person is advanced with their spiritual perceptive abilities they can experience Visions – like video clips or photos in detail and in colour. These are usually accompanied by a sudden "Knowingness" of what the vision means. I see spiritual visions given to me by the Angels when giving people messages, and when experiencing premonitions.

Coincidences: An example of spiritual help from the Angels

Have you ever thought about Coincidences?

Have you ever been thinking about someone and then shortly afterwards you meet them by chance? This can happen when you don't expect someone to be in a certain place, or perhaps you haven't seen that person for a long time. You can probably recall other coincidences in your personal life. Often what seems like coincidences are happenings brought about by the Guardian Angels for a reason.

The following is just one of many coincidences in my life:

I was driving home from work on a familar main road that I travel many times each week. My thoughts drifted to a story of a lady who had recently had a collision with a lorry carrying a large mobile home on a trailer. These vehicles are wide loads and overhang the carriageway of oncoming traffic. This incident resulted in her car hitting the overhanging mobile home. It sliced her car roof clean off. The mobile home lorry driver didn't even notice the collision and carrried on without stopping. Fortunately she wasn't injured but her car was a write-off.

So, here was I driving home when, minutes later, a lorry hauling a trailer with a large mobile home overhanging my carriageway appeared travelling towards me. I had to pull my car in to the edge of the road to avoid a collision. I realised then that my Guardian Angel had given me a warning. However, even with my high level of perception, I hadn't realised that my thoughts of a previous incident experienced by the lady had been triggered by my Guardian Angel. I write elsewhere in this book that our Guardian Angels communicate into our mind so completely that we may simply think of them as our own thoughts.

The Work of Guardian Angels

There are many different types of work that Angels do: Guiding, Healing, Guarding, bringing messages and visions, and warnings in the form of premonitions. Our main Guardian Angel accompanies us before birth, throughout life, and when passing back to Heaven at the end of our physical life.

One of the main areas of work for Guardian Angels is in guiding people towards a positive, fulfilling Life Plan. Our Guardian Angels were with us before our birth, whilst in Heaven, and know our intended Life Plan. It might be hard to believe that, for all of us, the Angelic Beings in Heaven plan our future life to be positive and fulfilling. Our everyday life is governed by our Free Will, but Heaven does plan some things for us, including soulmates that we might meet, positive events in our life, the type of work that we might do, where we might travel and live, and our interests. There will also be planned life challenges to help us spiritually grow. Life challenges are tough but are not meant to be beyond our capabilities. We may grow in spiritual maturity much quicker when we experience times of difficulties in life. Heaven seems to want as many people as possible to learn and grow from our life experiences so that we may become more caring to others, to nature, and the environment. However, Heaven also allows our Free Will to make our own choices in how we live our lives.

Our Guardian Angels try to lead us by communicating through our intuitive feelings. This might seem idyllic nonsense because, as we all know, there is much evil in this world, and we might immediately say: "Where are the loving Guardian Angels when people suffer serious illness, when people are so cruel, and when countries go to war?"

Human beings often become detached from their Guardian Angels, usually when they are self-centred, and lacking in empathy. When we are detached from our Guardian Angels our positive Life Plan will not happen, and we may feel let down by life, stressed, and lacking in life fulfilment. Those who lack empathy can also cause a huge amount of pain and destruction to people around them. If a Guardian Angel tries to communicate into a person's intuitive feelings to show empathy in a situation, then it is easy for many people to just ignore such feelings. Eventually, they create a barrier within that their Guardian Angel cannot get through. Self-centred lack of empathy can drive the soul of those who gain power over people, over countries, companies, or other groups that they control. The more they hurt people, the more evil, negative energy they seem to draw-in to influence their soul, accelerating the hurt that they cause.

This is one of the major causes of human suffering on planet Earth and also leads to human beings causing damage to nature and the environment.

One of the purposes of this book is in explaining how to recognise and be guided by the messages that our Guardian Angels communicate to us.

Our Guardian Angels also bring healing. The following is a true account:

Claire was aged in her forties and lived on her own in a rural location. It was late autumn when she fell ill with influenza. After about a week she was feeling weak and her breathing became difficult with a chest infection. She saw her doctor who prescribed rest and antibiotics and advised that she take some tests because he suspected that she had pneumonia. She went home and spent the next week in bed. She felt too weak to return to the doctor's surgery for tests. She knew she could call an ambulance for hospital treatment but felt happier staying at home. During a period of four days whilst she laid in bed, very unwell, a figure of an Angel appeared by her bedside. The Angel stayed with her for the four days, but no words were said. Claire just knew intuitively that this was her Guardian Angel bringing healing to her. After four days she began to feel better, and knew that she was past the most dangerous part of her illness. It was several weeks before she fully recovered, but knew from that moment on that Guardian Angels are real and bring healing to us through their unconditional love.

Learning to sense messages from the Angels means learning to become open to spiritual energies. Being "Spiritually Open", means having the ability to see, feel and sense these energies. Most people are not born Open because of the danger of being open to negative spiritual energies that are so prevalent on the Earth plain. To protect us from negative energies it seems that our memories of Heaven are deliberately blanked off at birth. This also means that most people are not open to the positive spiritual energies from our Guardian Angels that take the form of helpful messages, healing, positive feelings, enhanced intuition, conscience and love.

We can learn to sense our Guardian Angels and recognise the help that they constantly try to give us through messages and healing energies. We might experience a new awareness of Heaven. This can lead us onto a path of enlightenment so that we live our lives with less fear of our mortality, experience physical and mental healing, and greater financial security and life fulfilment. If we learn how to become "In Tune" with our Guardian Angel, we will find a wonderful positive change in our life.

Learning to blank our thoughts for a few minutes

When we blank our thoughts for just a short while, provided it is safe to do so, we are starting on a path of sensing our Guardian Angel. This is not the same as meditation because we need to blank our thoughts whilst still observing the world around us, looking for the feint spiritual energies which manifest at the edge of our perception. We live in a time of the most unusual experiences of being human. Many of us work with our brain, our mind, working with a computer screen in front of us. The introduction of smart phones and the emergence of social media leads to many of us occupying every spare moment. We may worry about everything, including relationships, family, health problems, finances, lack of self-fulfilment, career, exams, and all the challenges that life throws at us. We are bombarded by advertising everywhere we turn. We have no spare time in our minds from morning to late evening. Our Guardian Angels cannot be sensed when our minds are busy. No wonder so few people can sense or even believe in Angels.

When I was young, I used to lay awake at night worrying about anything that was currently a problem in my life. I remember lying in bed, unable to sleep, when one night I sensed my Guardian Angel giving me a vision. I could see myself from above. I was looking down at myself with a realisation that "Here I am in bed. It is night-time. What on Earth can I do about my problems right now? What can I achieve lying here, worrying? Isn't it better to get some sleep and then I can tackle my problems tomorrow without being tired?" I then got out of bed, made a note of my problems by writing them down. That cleared my mind. Writing our problems down transfers them out of our thoughts temporarily. With my mind now at rest I fell asleep quickly and easily. The next day, not only did I feel more refreshed, but my problems seemed to be resolved and go away.

Exercise

If you can find a few minutes to stop in your busy life, allow yourself some quiet time. Don't have tv, computers, mobile phones, or radio nearby. Ideally be on your own, in a quiet place. Write down your current problems that might be racing around your brain. Your brain deliberately fires current problems at the forefront of your mind as a survival mechanism. It's as though we are still living a primitive existence and our brain looks on challenges as real physical situations that we need to have in our immediate thoughts. So, when your brain is worrying about finances or anything else, it isn't your inner soul doing this, so write down anything you don't want to forget and allow yourself a few minutes of thinking nothing. It might take some practice. This is the first stage in allowing yourself to become more sensitive to the spiritual energies of your Guardian Angel.

My spiritual research started following the death of my grandfather. I asked questions to my family and friends about whether we survive physical death. No-one could give me an answer, so I started attending Christian Churches to find out what they believe. I attended Anglican Church services and study groups. Later, I attended Pentecostal services, Catholic Services, and Methodist services, eventually training as a Methodist preacher. I was baptised with an Anglican Church, a Pentecostal Church, and later confirmed at a Methodist Church. I led over one hundred services as a Methodist preacher during a four-year period 2000 to 2004.

Throughout my period as an active Christian, I continued with my spiritual research. My discoveries led me to a further understanding of Angels, especially our Guardian Angels. I found I could receive messages via the Angels concerning loved ones who have passed. Such messages often include names and other detail that no-one else could know. I learnt how to pass these messages on to people to help them through bereavement grief. I also found that messages were being given to me to help people with worries, fears and problems in life. So, what was happening to me? I began to see all diffrent types of Angels and receive messages from them. I occasionally had visions of Heaven. These spiritual experiences were accompanied by incredible feelings of unconditional love from Heaven. I was still conducting my spiritual research and, with every experience of our Guardian Angels I would ask questions about the meaning of life. The answers were always given to me, and I began to build up a picture of Heaven.

My belief in God became stronger than ever because of the spiritual experiences. Yet I made my own decision to stand down from training as a Methodist preacher. I did not discuss my spiritual experiences with Christian colleagues because I knew I would be criticised. Visions of Angels and of Heaven are not accepted by many faiths. The basis of Christian learning is Holy Scripture in writings almost two thousand years ago. I will never criticise Holy Scripture because Christian beliefs are still a big part of who I am. People who have strong religious beliefs are best keeping to their faith because it is their strength.

In my logical, questioning mind, through my spiritual research, I have been seeking present day evidence of Heaven, of the Angels and the meaning of life. I felt that with over seven billion people alive on Earth today that there must be evidence surrounding us concerning Angels and Heaven. The media, through television, cinema, and in storytelling produce many dramas and films that present fictional stories about serious crime, horror, war, and the supernatural. Television "Soap Operas" are filled with arguments, crime and people acting in an evil way. All of these give negative spiritual energy too much emphasis in our lives. We need to give emphasis to the miraculous loving power of Heaven and the Angels that try to help us.

The spiritual research that led to me to see and communicate with the Angels gave me a wonderful gift that I want to share with those who are truly interested. This gift works in a way that is equal to the best psychics. The Angels bring messages from loved ones who have passed, including names. They show me the worries and problems around people and communicate helpful messages, guidance and healing. Angels sometimes give me premonitions of the future.

I am hopeful that at least some of the readers will learn to see the universe differently and gain an increase in spiritual awareness and knowledge of the Angels. Not only is this a wonderful life changing path, but in many ways the ability to sense messages from our Guardian Angels helps to make the world a better place. Heaven has given me permission to teach this knowledge so that the world can face future challenges with many more people living their daily lives, being guided by Heaven.

CHAPTER TWO

Spiritual Research

The clairvoyant experiences of seeing Angels, sensing their messages, and healing, and at times seeing through to Heaven are so wonderful that they are difficult to compare with the analytical spiritual research that I conducted over many years that brought me to the point of being clairvoyant.
However, I must start at the same beginning that I had through the early years of my research.

Firstly, it is important to emphasise that the picture of the universe that I describe will, if taken seriously, lead to positive results in our spiritual perception and understanding of Angels.

One of my first areas of study was in that of belief versus knowledge. During the past two hundred years science has made discoveries that have changed the world. The discoveries are based on scientific facts that can be proven through real life experiments. Thoughout our education systems science, mathematics and other subjects are taught in way that we can believe and accept this knowledge. Our educational systems have shaped us into whom we are. I will not criticise this because human beings are geared to seek knowledge and new experiences. These driving forces are a natural part of being human.

Spiritual beliefs cannot be proven. Many people hold religious beliefs because they feel inside that we are a soul in a human body and that there is a Higher Authority who can be named God.

Holy Scripture gives accounts of times when humanity experienced miracles and that some gifted people were given great spiritual knowledge. In our modern world it would seem that present day religious experiences and miracles are not to be generally believed. Many religions teach the ancient Holy Scriptures but through the structure of their faith cannot accept modern day miracles and messages from Heaven. This leaves many people who are living in the modern world unable to fully believe in religious teachings.

Through my research I set about looking for evidence of our spirituality in the real time of "Now". I was surprised beyond words as my spiritual wareness and perception improved and subsequently resulted in me becoming clairvoyant.

Stage One: Looking at the world around differently

1) Our education systems teach that scienctific discoveries must be capable of proof. Spiritual discoveries cannot be proven by science. This meant that my research knowledge could only be built up on logical conclusions derived from the evidence of human experiences. Should many people, in different countries, and across different time periods record similar experiences then I conclude that the experiences will be those of real phenomena.

2) The limitation of our senses. Our physical senses cannot perceive so many things. The invisible energies of radio waves carrying mobile phone signals, radio and television cannt be detected by our senses. Gravity is invisible and so is electricity.

3) Life would not be possible but for the position of the Earth orbit and its axis (giving equal summer/, Also the gravitational influence of the Moon has been beneficial to life on Earth.

4) There has been a realisation in recent years, when studying climate, change just how the delicate and incredibly complex the

balance of life is in nature and the oceans.

Stage Two: Look at the nature of human beings

1) Emotions are these a spiritual quality?

2) Humanity has held beliefs in spirit/ God throughout history. Why, if we are merely biological creatures without a soul?

3) Why do human beings need to experience?: why not just build a dwelling, gather food, eat and vegetate?

4) Intelligence apart from the physical brain. Through many clairvoyant readings I have discovered that souls in Heaven keep all their memories and their personality.

5) Our soul is a conscious energy with a familiar home in Heaven

The spiritual realm of Heaven is another dimension, so a logical conclusion is that science will not be able to detect physical evidence of Heaven with scientific instruments. So-called spiritual experiences that people report should be taken seriously and compared with spiritual experiences reported by other people, perhaps living in other countries and from other cultures.

My research eventually gave me a detailed picture of the meaning of life. It emerged as a picture that made sense and could be explained logically. I had to abandon some, but not all my religious beliefs concerning the human soul and Heaven. As I began to see the universe differently, I began to sense and see the Angels, and I could sense the energies from Heaven. The certainty that I had in understanding the basic meaning of life meant that I could sense Angel energies interacting with all of us and I knew that I could trust those energies completely.

So, an important prerequisite to sensing and communicating with the Angels from Heaven is to acquire an understanding that our inner self is a conscious eternal soul whose true home is in the spiritual dimension of conscious energy, Heaven.

It might surprise many people to be told that learning Clairvoyance is not done by meditating or looking for answers without any focus from within ourselves. The first, important, technique is in learning to observe the world around, observe people and look out for feint spiritual energies at the periphery of our perception. We are learning to have spiritual experiences in this very moment of "Now". That is what clairvoyance is all about: it is experiencing spiritual phenomena in a state of heighten ed awareness, heightened alertness, that is good and positive and given to us in a Divine way "Now".

An acquaintance of mine is a psychic and medium and was born as a gypsy. In adult life he served in the army and later became an outdoor survival teacher for the army. At the age of just seven years his parents had him employed in giving readings to the public. The instruction to him was "Just say what comes into your head". To any rational person such an instruction doesn't make sense. However, through my spiritual research listening to what comes into our head in the moment of "Now" can, very cautiously, be taken more seriously. This is because we all have a Guardian Angel who tries to communicate with us.

A Further Exercise in blanking our Thoughts

The exercise involves clearing away the constant stream of thoughts and worries racing around in our head. To do this we need to blank our thoughts for just a few minutes and tell ourselves that we can recommence our worries afterwards!

One way of blanking thoughts is to sit quietly, yet remain alert, and bring our attention to the immediate moment, the instant of right now. So, close your eyes and, for just one minute, listen to any sounds in the room, or from outside. After one minute recall the sounds that you heard. If you were doing this right, you would notice that your mind is brought into an awareness of the present moment in time.

The next part of the exercise can be performed in one of two ways. If you have someone in your mind who has passed across to Heaven, think about them but only do this where there was a bond of close friendship or love. If not, just think that you would like to sense your Guardian Angel.

Again, close your eyes and concentrate on the sounds you might hear in the area you are seated. Move your thoughts to this person and say a short prayer to Heaven to give you just one word as a message via your Guardian Angel. You most likely will not hear a word as a voice. The word is usually received intuitively, as if suddenly from nowhere a word has been put into your thoughts. The word might not be identifiable so keep sitting quietly and try to sense intuitively how many syllables in the word, One? Two? Three? What is the first letter or first sound in pronunciation of the word? What do you feel is the actual word? Remember "Just say what comes into your head".

At this point you might feel slightly excited with the experience, or you might feel nothing at all. If so, keep on practising this important exercise. I estimate at this point around 10% of readers will see some success with this. If you feel positive, ask for further words, then sit back and see if the message makes sense. The Guardian Angels will often send words to help you with a current worry or problem in your life.

How will we see Angels?

I do not see Angels all the time. When my soul has been given a vision of Heaven, I have been able to see Angels. I am spiritually grounded and do not see Angels when I am at work or when my mind is occupied by entertainment such as watching tv. At times in life when I have been ill, I have seen them. Angels intensify their energies when they are channelling healing to a person, an animal and to damaged areas of nature and this results in them becoming more visible.

I have seen Angels appearing as flashes of light in woodland and I have asked the Angels "What are you doing?". The Angels would reply be telling me that healing energies were being channelled for animals, birds, wildflowers and trees. When I channel healing for a person, I see Angels who are bringing-in healing energies shimmering in different colours depending on the type of healing needed. I see them visibly because they have intensified their healing energies and projected them into the physical dimension.

What do Angels Look Like?

There are many ways that humans describe how Angels appear and what they look like. Angels can appear just as might be expected by the person who experiences a vision of an Angel. In other words, they can change their appearance.

I see Guardian Angels without wings, as beautiful male, or female Beings. I see all other Angels with what appears to be wings, dressed in robes and radiating light. The light that they radiate, almost as the sun, could be mistaken for wings, especially as visions of Angels often appear suspended in mid-air. They are of another dimension and not affected by gravity.

I am always drawn to the face of an Angel. Their loving eyes tell you that they know everything about you, your good, your bad, and the mistakes you may have made in life. It can be sensed that you are loved unconditionally by Heaven for whom you are.

How do we sense Angels?

For myself, whereas I do not see Angels all the time, I do sense my Guardian Angel with me all the time. I sense a gentle warmth, and a feeling of being accompanied through life, and a reassurance that Heaven isn't far away.

When I was young, I didn't sense Angels and didn't know what to believe about Heaven. I had much to learn. As experienced by many, many people I went through times when I was lonely, perhaps mildly depressed and feeling cold inside. I believe that learning to sense Angels will help people, so that they have fewer times of feeling cold and lonely,

How do Angels communicate with us?

Angels communicate in many ways. They might give us a sign, a coincidence, or something unusual that we can take as being a message. They communicate through our intuition, and our conscience. They might give us intuitive feelings that are warnings to avoid travel or avoid doing something. Angels might communicate with an inner voice, but mostly through an intuitive "Sudden knowingness" in our mind. What they communicate to us will always be positive and will never involve hurting others or hurting ourselves.

How do we communicate with Angels?

Angels sense our needs and our life problems, so it is not always necessary to communicate with them. When I need special help such as a way forward through overwhelming problems, I make a prayer to the Highest Spiritual Authority in Heaven, to God. The prayer must be made with the purpose of opening a way forward that will not hurt others. Angels work in the purpose of Heaven, and such a prayer, if made with goodness in our heart, is powerful because the Angels act in the purpose of God. Having come from a Christian background I always make a Christian prayer.

Negative Energies

Negative energy is spiritual energy that is the opposite to the energies of Heaven. The energies from Heaven are positive, and creative energies. Negative energies hurt people, hurt nature, and hurt the environment. They are not creative but destructive.

People who hurt others physically or psychologically are working in a negative way. Self-centred people mostly don't care about others, because they just think about themselves. A lack of empathy and care indicates a spiritually immature soul. If a person constantly hurt others, then they risk opening themselves up spiritually to negative Earthbound energies. Once negative spiritual energies start to influence a person who lacks empathy then that person will often become worse in their cruel behaviour towards others.

Sometimes people self-harm. This is because they are influenced by negative spiritual energies that want to cause harm. Such a person might say hurtful things to those who care about them. They may also self-harm or behave in an odd way because negative energy seeks to destroy and hurt them.

What is Negative energy?

The human soul has free will to be good or bad in life. Spiritually immature souls are self-centred and more likely to cause hurt. They want money, possessions, and control of others, and are often lacking in empathy. They do not want to understand or care about how others feel at hurt they cause.

Hurting others indicates that a person has a low level of spiritual resonance. When a person behaves in this way then they become almost disconnected from their Guardian Angel. Our Guardian Angel tries to protect us from evil, negative spiritual energies. Once we disconnect from our Guardian Angel then we become spiritually like an open door for the destructive negative energies to influence us.

The influence of negative energies will gradually darken our soul energy. Our soul energy is like a light that surrounds our soul inner core of the "I am". When we pass across to Heaven after physical life, we shed the dark soul energy and it is left behind on the Earth plain. Unfortunately, the dark soul energies that have been left behind by many millions of people is like a reservoir of negative energy, sometimes concentrated in small pockets, and in some ways everywhere. Negative energy is never far away and ready to influence anyone who disconnects from their Guardian Angel because they have been hurting others or nature on a repeated basis.

Having given readings to many thousands of people where I passed on messages from the Angels, almost everyone I have helped found that the messages provided evidence of survival of the soul of a loved one beyond physical death.

At the time of receiving messages, I was invariably overwhelmed by the beauty of the experience and the positive benefit to the person whom I was helping. For me, every time of messages is a time of being close to the Angels and seems like a miracle, as it was for most of the people whom I helped. Modern day miracles really can happen. Only afterwards would my enquiring mind think through what had happened. My first thought was usually: "What have I learnt about Heaven from the experience?"

Every time I receive messages, I find the experience to be as different as each of the people I helped. The messages always show me evidence of Heaven from different perspectives, for every person has their own spiritual way of relating to Heaven.
I can understand the religious descriptions of Heaven as being "Holy" with teachings of spiritual love.
The unconditional LOVE in Heaven really is an energy, and that energy is something we need to feel as a part of our natural soul state. We can experience and be a part of that LOVE without religious beliefs.
I can look at Heaven in a mystical way, yet also in a matter-of-fact way, as another dimension that must have its own laws of physics. Above all else the spiritual dimension of Heaven is a place of infinite intelligence. It is the place of what I call "Conscious Energy". Our soul, the real "I" or "Me" inside all of us is made of the same Conscious Energy. Heaven is our familiar, friendly, true home from where we came before birth, and where we return after our physical life as a human being comes to an end.
I know that Heaven wanted me to help people with my gift of seeing and sensing the Angels. Heaven continues to give me visions and messages via the Angels.

When we are receiving messages from Angels we are not speaking to the dead. Communication with Heaven is simply to receive visions and messages from the Angels.
Whenever I do a reading, I realise that I cannot speak with those who have passed. The Guardian Angels from Heaven give me a vision of the person in spirit, and it is the same Angels that give me messages from the deceased soul. Sometimes the person I am giving a reading seeks to ask questions. I have to tell them that I find that I cannot ask questions because they will not be answered. Yet, surprisingly the deceased soul, communicating

through the Angels would invariably give me messages for the person that were the most important ones. It was as if Heaven knew the questions that were burning inside of the heart of the person I was reading.

Those souls that have been allowed into Heaven, by the Grace of God are not dead to sin, but very much alive in their soul state. The big surprise to myself as I progressed through many thousands of readings to help people who are mostly non-religious, is that most people make it through to a place I name "First Heaven" even if their life was less than perfect. The lives of many people are less than perfect, we all make mistakes in life.

Life Review

In Heaven we will all be accompanied by our Guardian Angel to experience a "Life Review" where we will be shown the good things we achieved and see the hurt that we have caused others. It is only truly evil people who do not make it to Heaven, usually by their own choice, because they realise that their life review will not be easy. Such evil and tormented souls sometimes choose to stay Earthbound for a while, often manifesting as ghosts or poltergeists. Eventually all these souls are gathered up to be dealt with by Heaven, but not before they have caused some fear and upset as evil earthbound energies.

My training as a Christian preacher did give me the important spiritual gift of "Discernment". This is a true ability to differentiate between good and evil spirits. I can block communication with evil spirits, and only allow the Angels from Heaven to give me messages. I know some clairvoyants who allow any spiritual energy to communicate with them. This can be dangerous, and I believe that this is what Holy Scripture refers to as "It is a sin to speak to the dead". Negative, evil energies do exist in small earthbound pockets, usually attached to a house, historic building, or an area of land. They frequently make the most of being able to manifest, causing unnerving physical disturbances using negative spiritual energies. The overwhelming majority of souls do make it safely to First Heaven, yet once in Heaven then their ability to communicate with those still in life seems almost impossible other than through messages from the Angels. I believe that Heaven respects the right of those in life to live without interference from spirits, good or bad.

TUNING IN TO HEAVEN

As I previously explained this book is not about religion. I am a spiritual researcher and I constantly look for logical explanations before I come to tentative conclusions. My very real spiritual experiences that subsequently came from my spiritual research have given me personal proof of Heaven and the Angels.

Many people use the term "Afterlife" as a general description for a life that our soul will move on to after our physical life ends.

The term "Afterlife" embraces all possible spiritual experiences after we leave our physical life. In my research I have discovered that most souls reach Heaven, even though their lives may have been far from perfect. Perhaps one person in a thousand might choose not to go directly to Heaven because of some traumatic end to their life or because of evil deeds that they committed in life. Negative, evil energy does exist on the earth plane in pockets, whereas Heaven is infinite.

Heaven is another dimension where love is felt as a real, natural energy. It is our familiar true home where we came from before birth. Heaven is a separate place, but it is also all around us. We are surrounded in life by spiritual energies that most people are quite blind to. Some of the energies are negative, evil energies which is why we should never open ourselves up to evil. Often, when a person does bad things, such as hurting others, they find it easy to feed off negative energies that seem to boost their ability to continue doing bad things.

I will explain how we can learn to discern between negative energies and the energies of Heaven. By tuning into the Angels and the energies of Heaven we can access the most powerful help.

If we learn to tune in to Heaven the benefits are life changing. We may lose the fear of our mortality. We may begin to access true spiritual guidance and help from Heaven. Those in Heaven whom we call "Guardian Angels" simply try to help us through life. They communicate through our feelings, our intuition and our conscience. They try to bring healing to us. They can also help us see the future in some significant ways, and more importantly change our futures for the better.

Learning to "Tune-in" to Heaven helps us be closer to our Guardian Angel. With an open mind, determination and love for others and nature we may discover a gradual move forward in life towards Heaven-sent spiritual empowerment beyond our wildest dreams!

Exercise

When you can find time to sit quietly, then try the following Visualisation:

Close your eyes and imagine yourself in a dark room. The room has no windows, and the door is closed. There is no light, and you realise that all Is completely black. You are feeling as if you are floating in a dark void.

Now imagine the door slightly open. An intense, beautiful light shines through the opening and starts to drive away the darkness. The door opens further, and the beautiful light now fills the room. Outside all you can see is Light.

Now, feel yourself moving out of the door outside into the Light. There is nothing to see only Light surrounding you. You are relaxed and sense a gentle warmth. The energy you notice and start to feel is that of unconditional love within the Light and surrounding you.

Keep drifting forward in the Light, and before you visualise a garden full of flowers, radiating every colour. Feel yourself drawn into the garden and visualise the beauty of the flowers surrounding you.

At the head of the garden, visualise an Angel. Flowing robes of white, radiating and shimmering with energy. Find yourself drawn to the face of the Angel and look at the eyes of the Angel, looking at you with unconditional love. You realise that you are loved for whom you are, all the good, and all the mistakes.

In your visualisation stay in this garden with your Guardian Angel for as long as you wish. When you are ready, pull out of the visualisation, open your eyes and just sit relaxing for a few minutes.

You might need to read through the visualisation several times before you try it. Alternatively, you could ask someone who you know is interested to narrate the visualisation gently and slowly.

Summary of the Exercise

Yes, you have just used your imagination for this exercise. However, the visualisation is a real example of entering the Light of Heaven. It is a building block in opening-up your spiritual awareness of Angels. Success rate in this exercise averages 50%. Unsuccessful averages 25% of people honestly saying that they are incapable of visualising, and the final 25% saying that visualising was easy, but they didn't feel anything spiritually.

CHAPTER THREE

See the Universe Differently

During the early years of my research, I made an amateur study of Quantum Physics, and was fascinated by the theories of parallel universes, and observations that the tiniest particles of matter appeared to behave in strange ways. At sub-atomic level, the tiniest particles of matter can appear from nowhere and disappear into seemingly nowhere.

I began to visualise solid objects around me in a different way. Everything is made of unimaginable vast amounts of energy within the atoms. Invisible energy that holds things together. I could look at a wooden table, and then visualise it as semi-transparent with nothing in between the atoms and molecules except invisible energy.

I thought about radio and television signals travelling through the air at the speed of light, carrying vast amount of information, yet we see and feel nothing unless we have equipment that can convert these signals back into video and audio.

I read that Quantum Physics has a theory that is named "The Spooky Theory". An electron can cause another electron at the other side of the universe to instantly move in the same way at the same time. We make use of the Spooky Theory when speaking on the phone, when using apps, and when using any computerised device. Have you ever questioned how messaging, or use of apps is an instantaneous process? Most people just accept these things without asking questions.

All these observations show us that our physical senses are quite limited. Our eyes pick-up light, our ears pick-up sound. Then we have the senses of smell, taste and touch, and that's it!
I began to realise that we can't see, hear, touch, smell or taste spiritual energies that are very real.

Who or what are we?
Our soul energy is made of the same stuff that I call "Conscious Energy" that populates Spiritual Realm of "Heaven". This is nothing spooky or weird, and nothing to be frightened about because Heaven is our true home.

An important gift when learning to sense Angels is the gift of Discernment between good spiritual energies, and negative, evil spiritual energies. Sometimes evil can often show itself as good so the ability to truly discern is an acquired skill that must be gradually developed.

There are spiritual energies around us all the time, mainly from the Angels, helping, guiding, and constantly trying to heal and sustain life, including ourselves.
Spiritual energies sustain life and are simply named as "Life Energies". I believe that Life Energies are programmed – like a computer operating system. Our body is the "Hardware", and our everyday tasks are the "Application Software" or "Apps". Life Energies keep our body working and bring-in healing.

In our everyday experience as human beings we may not notice the faint spiritual energies at the outer edge of our perception.
With enhanced knowledge of Heaven, and the Angels we can look out for these energies and learn the first steps in recognising them.
There is an almost impenetrable barrier between the Spiritual Realm, and the physical universe in which we are temporarily in

life dwelling. I say "Almost" because there are energies there that we can, with the correct knowledge, recognise, interpret, and respond to.

Much of the spiritual activity that can be sensed is from the Angels, especially our own Guardian Angels.

Sensing Angels: Many people Question "Are We Spiritual?"

The most basic questions are all connected: Are we spiritual? Is there a Heaven? Is there any form of spiritual afterlife?

Science tells us that we do not have a soul and that a Heaven cannot exist because science is unable to find evidence that these exist. The most common ways that human beings can accept that there is a spiritual dimension and that we ourselves have a soul are through either religious beliefs or personal spiritual experiences. In modern times so called "Near Death Experiences" have become widely recorded. This is because many people who have been near death due to injury or serious illness have been saved by modern day professional medical help. During their time at the closest point to death some estimates indicate that around 17% of people experience an out-of-body spiritual event that can be recalled later. These NDE experiences can be totally convincing and life changing. Sometimes those experiencing an NDE can recall seeing their Guardian Angel.

The following is an account of a NDE based on a true experience: Peter was proud of his motor bike and travelled everywhere on it, including travel to work. Kate, his girlfriend ,constantly worried about him riding his bike because he seemed oblivious to danger, especially in bad weather situations. The day that he had his accident was a weekend and he decided to visit his parents who lived nine miles away from his home. The weather was quite bad with heavy rain and strong winds as he travelled on a country road out of town. His bike suddenly hit a bump in the road that knocked his steering. The bike started to swerve uncontrollably on the wet road surface. He came off the road and hit a tree and everything went black.

Peter found himself awake in hospital. He was looking down at a hospital bed with a doctor and two nurses attending someone who was unconscious. It took him a moment to realise that the person they were attending was himself. He didn't feel concerned, nor did he feel afraid. He felt good and yet he knew what the doctor and nurses were thinking. The nurses were thinking "He won't make it. He is going to die". The doctor was thinking "I will try my best to save him".

Peter found himself being drawn to a light at the side of the room. The light seemed warm and inviting as he entered its loving embrace. He was moving at high speed in what seemed like a tunnel at the end of which was the source of the light. He could see the vague outline of two people stood in the light. Suddenly he found himself in a calm, beautiful meadow. The grass was green, and flowers of every shade seemed to shine with a vivid intensity that left him lost for words. Peter was surprised at how he felt. All his senses were working yet he had no physical body. His soul energy was his body. He felt as though this was the true reality of home. Unconditional love was around him like the air that he had breathed in life. Peter also experienced a profound feeling of oneness with the universe.

He was met by his grandma who he knew had died last year. His grandad was stood with her. He had died nine years earlier. "It is not your time," said his grandma. Peter felt totally unconcerned about the life he had just left. "Can I stay here?" said Peter. His grandma did not reply, but then a spiritual being appeared, in the form of person and yet radiating light. He felt that this was an Angel. The Angel had no wings and appeared with white and purple radiant garments and a presence that felt loving but strict, with some spiritual authority. "You have things to do that we planned for you in your life. You must go back", said the Angel. "Are you my Guardian Angel?" asked Peter. Before he received a response, he suddenly felt himself much heavier and began to feel some discomfort and pain. He opened his eyes and realised that he was back in his body in a hospital bed. A nurse saw that he had regained consciousness and he heard her say to a colleague "He is awake, thank goodness, I thought we had lost him".

Peter eventually made a full recovery although he never rode a motor bike again. He was reluctant to tell people about his NDE, but he did tell his girlfriend Kate. Kate was the person who told me about this when she came to me for Angel messages. During the consultation I was given a message that her boyfriend had been injured in a motor incident and that it had changed his life. She confirmed to me that Peter had experienced this life changing event and that it had made him more caring towards her and others. Peter was no longer scared at the thought of death, but now knew that it was only the beginning of another stage in the eternal life of his true inner being.

The following is a further true account of an NDE, but a different experience:

Alison was on holiday with her sister at a popular seaside holiday resort on the south coast of England. The weather was hot and sunny, so they headed for the beach. There were lifeguard stations so the two felt totally at ease as they walked into the sea. "I'll race you swimming up to that buoy" said her sister Carol. The buoy floated bright orange about two hundred yards off the beach. It was probably something securing a fishing pot for catching lobsters or crabs. Alison reached the buoy first and turned to see Carol approaching her and looking frustrated because she came second. The girls, both aged in their twenties, held position together at the buoy. "The water is cold!" shouted Alison. "Come on let's get back to the beach and warm up in the sun". "You go first" she said to Carol. "I will still try to win".

Carol lunged forward to swim towards the beach in the cold sea water. Alison waited a few seconds then struck forward to swim back. Suddenly her arms and legs went into severe cramp. The shock of the cold sea was hitting her. She struggled to keep swimming but the harder she tried the more her arms and legs screamed with pain. She could no longer swim and found herself being submerged. She tried to get her head above water and screamed for help. The cold sea started to swallow her. It seemed quite deep and small waves that she hadn't really noticed were hindering her attempts to gasp a mouthful of air. She realised she was drowning and going under. Her senses of panic overwhelmed her. In her mind her life flashed before her. Every minute of her life could be vividly seen, ending in her sadness at the memory of her daughter, now aged two years, at home with her partner Mike who was at home while she took a day out with her sister.

The pain in her limbs disappeared and then she felt herself in a place of blackness. She couldn't understand what has happened to her but didn't feel frightened. A small light appeared in the distance, racing towards her and getting bigger as it approached. The light quickly reached her, and she felt at ease and surrounded by light. The light enveloped like a warm blanket of love as she saw in the light an Angel and her father who had died the previous year. The Angel looked on with love as her father gave her a message: "It's not your time Alison. Tell your mother I love her and that I still watch over her". Another beautiful Angel then came into view. Without words she knew it was her Guardian Angel who knew everything about her, her good and bad, and loved her unconditionally for whom she was and is.

The moment on the edge of Heaven came to and ended as she awoke coughing up sea water, gasping for breath. She felt cold like she had never been before, and her breathing was painful. She was alive. The lifeguards had been quick to act when they heard her screams before she went under the water. Carol was with her and held her hand as she was taken by stretcher into an ambulance and then on to the local A&E hospital.

After an overnight stay in hospital Alison made a full recovery.

Many months later she came to see me for Angel messages. Her father came through and her Guardian Angel brought through a vision of this incident that Alison confirmed as correct. Her life had been changed forever by her near-death experience and she felt spiritually stronger. Alison was happy and deeply moved emotionally to hear messages from her father.

As with most people who have experienced an NDE she now

seemed to value every moment of every day as a blessing and life as a precious gift. Her experience of life flashing before her eyes as she was drowning has led to questions in my spiritual research. This is quite a common experience.

Question to Heaven: "Why do some people see their life flashing before them at the time of near death?

Message from Heaven: "The human brain has a memory and so does the spiritual soul of a person. At the time of near death, the brain is programmed to upload as much memory as possible to the soul. The memory bank of life experiences is important to the soul as the person transitions back from physical life to Heaven. The brain is one of the first organs to die. Again, this is by deliberate design so that the soul of a person can be released quickly when life in the physical body is at an end.

My preferred description of our soul is "Conscious Energy". Our soul is made of this energy and the spiritual dimension is that of Conscious Energy.

The main spiritual dimension of what we may describe as "Heaven" is one where the energy of love is at its greatest natural state. Love can be just an emotion but in its purest form Love is an energy. The dimension of Heaven is almost infinite. The opposite to love is negative energy, or in its worst form it is described as evil. Negative energy is earthbound and exists in small, localised pockets.

CHAPTER FOUR

Learn how Angels help Us

Angels may give us visions through our Spiritual "Third Eye"
When learning to sense Angels it is beneficial to learn how to interpret images that come into our mind. Are such images generated from our inner memories, or, if images are unexpected, are they spiritual?
The Third Eye is not a physical eye, it is our spiritual eye.
When we see images in our mind then these can be memories that have been stored by our brain and re-created as images.
If I said to you "Visualise a pace where you went on holiday", then you might see an image of that place in your mind's eye. The image would have been retrieved from the memory in your brain and brought instantly to the front of your mind.

Such images can also be held in our soul memory. I know this because every time the Angels bring messages from a loved one who has passed, they also give me images of almost anything they wish to communicate. These images are still held in the soul memory of the person now in Heaven, having been retained whilst they were in life.

If we allow ourselves to stop occasionally and blank our thoughts through mediation, then we might allow our third eye to pick up random images.
This is a spiritual time we might allow ourselves to not recall a holiday or anything else because we are deliberately not allowing ourselves to think about the past, present or future.
Of course, random images might not appear in our mind. After

all, why should any image appear when we have quietened our thoughts?

I always blank my mind of thoughts before I connect with the Angels to bring messages for someone. I clear my own thoughts completely and leave myself open to whatever my Angel Guide places in my mind. It could be an image of a deceased person who has a love connection with the person I am with, or a place, or an item of clothing, or anything. I would also, at the same time, receive messages that accompany the image as a sudden "Knowingness"

I will give some examples of how images might be given to me in my Third Eye:
If I am giving a reading, it is usually to connect with a loved-one who has passed. I would be given images by my Angel Guide, who will be working with the Guardian Angel of the person sat in front of me, and the Guardian Angel of the person in Heaven. The first image I am usually shown is the image of the person who has passed. Often, they appear at the side of the person I am reading. I am free to scan up and down the vision of the deceased person. I will usually start by describing whether I am seeing a male or female, old or young, with an approximate age. I can see their hairstyle, hair colour, and their face. I would see if they wore much make-up, and describe dress jewels such as a ring, or necklace.

I am often drawn to what they are wearing, and the colour and style of their clothing. Sometimes this can be comical, and the humour will be from the person in spirit who might admit to having worn the same slippers for many years, hence they seem well worn. I have had men in spirit deliberately show me an image of holes in their socks. This would have been true to life, and a genuine attempt by a person in spirit to reassure that the Heaven is not without laughter, but a place where we can retain a sense of humour. Indeed, the clairvoyant readings consistently show that we retain our character in the Heaven. This is because we are all unique, and our character is not just our brain, but our inner, eternal soul that we call "Me" or "I"

.

Current Life Help from Angels

When I receive Angel messages concerning the current life problems and difficulties of someone then the person in front of me doesn't want to connect with a loved one who has passed. He or she is wanting to know if I can see what is happening in their life, and what can I tell them concerning their future. Again, my Angel Guide works with their Guardian Angel to give me messages that are relevant. I would see these as images that mean nothing to me, but when I describe what I see are of importance to the person in front of me. I am also given knowledge as a "Sudden Knowingness", and I hear words, especially names. I describe what I see and hear, and the messages from the Angels will progress from there.

When I say "Progress", I mean that I start to see images of their future, and I receive messages concerning their future.

When a person has told me nothing, except to confirm what I say, they are usually amazed about things I describe concerning their past and present life. However, I often tell them "Look, you have come to see me because you want to know what the future holds. Yes, I give thanks when the Angels give me messages about your past and present when I knew nothing about you, but you already know your past and present, so it is only worth seeing me if the Angels are willing to tell you about your future". I gave a young couple, Jim and Vickie and Angel messages reading. "I have been given a vision of a new home" I said. Vickie replied that they were living together in a small apartment and saving for a deposit for a new home. I then said: "I see a new car, a black BMW". "That's my new car", said Jim. Vickie then told me that he had spent his money on a new car when they were supposed to be saving for their house deposit. I then went on to give them both Angel messages concerning their careers, and messages from a paternal grandmother whose spirit is in

Heaven.

SENSING THE FUTURE

It seems amazing when a person with Psychic gifts gives a Fortune Telling Reading. We might think to ourselves "How do they do it".

In my spiritual research I question "How do such amazing thoughts come into the mind of a psychic?"

The answer is, of course, that someone is helping them. Most psychics would readily agree that it is their Spirit Guide who helps them. I only ever connect spiritually with Angels, especially our Guardian Angels.

Our Guardian Angels know our Life Plan. Yes, we all have a Life Plan determined in Heaven before we were born, and our Guardian Angels know our Life Plan, and know some of our future.

Our own Free Will is commonly understood to have led us to where we are today and defines our actions and future Life Events. My research has surprisingly led to the conclusion that future events on our Life Plan will happen irrespective of our daily free will decisions.

However, some people live lives without empathy and disconnect from sensing their Guardian Angel. Their future life could be way off course from that planned in Heaven. These are the people who cause damage and destruction on our planet.

Free will influences our daily routine yet, we can sacrifice some of our free will to another person when in a close relationship with them. We can sacrifice some of our free will by caring for someone and helping them in everyday tasks.

The Future is linked to the Past

The key discovery in my learning about how the Angels see the future was when I came to the realisation that much of the future is determined and planned in the past. What has been planned for us is then steered by our Guardian Angel into happening in immensely powerful spiritual ways to become our future reality.

However, this process is frequently prevented by our individual spiritual free will. If we don't understand, if we can't or don't want to listen to Heaven, then the good positive things planned for our personal future might not happen. Life then becomes a struggle that can last for many years, or even a lifetime.

The heading "Aspects of the Soul" explains in detail how we might receive guidance from Heaven, through our Guardian Angels trying to help and guide us.

How was our future life planned? This process is simply determining a "Life Plan". Our Life Plan seeks to remedy things that we need to correct, and to give us the opportunity to learn to enable our further spiritual development.

Past Lives

Most of us will have experienced life as another person prior to our present life. We may have had many lives. The person that we truly are inside, the "I" or "Me" has been shaped by previous lives. This "Shaping" contributes to our character and our driving forces in this life.

Firstly, it is essential that we identify our Driving Forces. We can ask ourselves questions such as: "Am I adventurous or shy? Am I outgoing or not? Do I enjoy challenges or not? Am I outspoken?"

Secondly, we need to accept that we have a Life Plan, which was determined before we were born. We all have a Life Plan that our Guardian Angels know. We need to learn to listen to our

Guardian Angels to help identify our Life Challenges that were included in the Life Plan.

What was planned for our future can often be perceived by taking seriously the inner visions of who we always wanted to be, and our inner thoughts of what we always wanted to do.

Our Guardian Angels try to help us by gently steering us forward on our Life Plan. They do this by working through our intuitive feelings, although whether or not a person listens to their intuition is examined in detail in the next chapter "Aspects of the Soul".

Our Guardian Angels accompany
us and continue to help us
when our physical life ends

After physical death our soul can be eager to give a sign to a loved one left behind that they still exist, that their true inner self survived and has now found peace. This is quite a common occurrence, usually happening before a funeral takes place. It would seem that our Guardian Angels can allow us to be close to loved ones such as family and friends during the days before the funeral. This won't happen if we don't want it, or if loved ones would be spooked by spiritual signs. Although quite a common occurrence, any signs from the deceased soul are only occasionally picked up and recognised. There follows some true accounts of this phenomena. Although these accounts are amazing, what is even more amazing to me is that someone who has suffered prolonged illness can quickly accept that they have died and seemingly adapt almost immediately to their soul state. Of course, it is our Guardian Angels who help the deceased soul to adapt, and help the soul in trying to give a sign to loved ones still in life.

True account with name changed

George awoke at six in the morning to see an apparition of his uncle at the foot of the bed. His uncle, although elderly, had been in good health. George looked on in amazement as his uncle spoke to him to say that he had just died following emergency admission to hospital. His uncle then went on to talk about his will. He told George to go to his house, into the bedroom and pull the bed forward to reveal a small hidden cupboard behind the bed. Inside the cupboard was a safe that contained his will. The uncle then explained where the safe key was hidden, and then the apparition disappeared.

Later that day George received a phone call from one of his cousins, a son of the uncle, to inform him of the death. George said nothing about the apparition. After the funeral George offered to help clear out the house of his uncle along with other family members. There had been a lot of concern that a will hadn't been found. George said nothing and made his way into the bedroom, and found the will in the hidden safe exactly as described by the apparition.

George told me, with a sense of humour, that he wasn't too concerned that when the will was read he hadn't been included as a beneficiary.

It would seem that the Guardian Angels had helped the uncle get a message through to a family member who was most receptive, in this case George.

I now give a very personal account of messages from my mother on the day of her passing. Family members had been with my father throughout the day. I went back to see him during the evening. Family members had left and he was sat alone in a distraught state. My mother had suffered with dementia for many years, with short term memory loss and deteriorating health.

My father said : "I have been looking for our wedding photograph all evening and I can't find it anywhere!". I knew that I couldn't be much help. My parents never allowed me to go anywhere except the lounge when I visited and no mention had ever been made of the wedding photo. Suddenly I heard the voice of my mother and I relayed the message to my father. "The wedding photo is in the third drawer down of the drawers at the foot of her bed". "I have already looked there" said my father, who then went into the bedroom, and sure enough, in the third drawer down was the missing wedding photo. My father was amazed, but the messages didn't stop there as my mother gave messages concerning the location of personal items of hers that my father would find comforting. In various hidden place my father found these special possessions of my mothers.

After all this my father said, with a smile on his face: "She is here, and I know that she has survived death. I can now accept that she is in a better place, and free of the distress of her terrible illness".

After that pivotal moment the rest of my family were amazed at how well Dad was handling the loss of our mother in a calm, positive way.

Looking at this miracle in an analytical way it can be seen the the Guardian Angels helped mother to quickly adapt to the Afterlife. I have consistently found, in giving many readings, that those who suffered dementia, or Alzheimer's disease recover their full normal personality after they have passed to the Afterlife. Their soul memories are intact up to a point where the disease resulted in short term memory loss. As explained elsewhere in this book, our soul memory retains the same information as our physical brain. I believe that the missing wedding photo had been stored in the third drawer in her bedroom suite for many years, a memory which her soul still retained.

CHAPTER FIVE

When I give people an Angel messages reading, they frequently comment that they sense a calm, healing atmosphere. My Angel Guide shows me a vision of those who are spiritually very much alive in Heaven and will pass on messages from loved ones. I am shown images of places and objects that may mean something to the person I am reading. I may also see what has happened, and what is happening in the lives of those whom I read and ask my Angel to show me the Life Path for that individual, to help them back on the correct path to fulfilment and happiness.

Angels help in the following ways: Angels speak to us through our intuition. Have you ever struggled with a problem, unable to find an answer, then suddenly the answer is there? Have you ever been overwhelmed by stress and worry, and then somehow you work through the situation? Have you ever had a gut feeling that you shouldn't go somewhere, and later discover that you are glad you listened to your intuition? .... or maybe you didn't listen to your intuition and regretted doing something? Your Guardian Angel helps you through your intuition. There is no language, just an instant awareness of what we should or shouldn't do by a form of telepathy which we don't acknowledge because we don't realise that we are being helped. In some people the fine tuning of their intuition can lead to an individual becoming in some ways clairvoyant. If we pray to God for healing, then a Healing Angel will help bring healing directly to the person suffering, both spiritually, and through those working to help medically.

Angels can be with us to give us STRENGTH. Both physical, and emotional strength.

A Prayer to God is essential. Angels can be with us to guide us through life's problems and difficulties.

Angels helping us in our daily lives can only be appreciated if we believe in God and the Angels.

A word of caution: Angels rarely communicate as a voice in your head unless to give a sudden warning of imminent danger. A voice in your head is not allowed because a voice telling us what to do would go against our "Free Will" to live our lives as we choose. Also, an Angel of God would never be a nuisance by bothering you in ways you don't want. Angels of God certainly never guide us with bad thoughts.

How can a belief in Angels help you?

If you can find somewhere quiet where you can spend a few minutes on your own. It could be just another room in your home. Sit quietly, relax, and try, just try to blank your mind and think of nothing for just one minute. What can you achieve by worrying about the past or future? So, sit quietly and try to appreciate the intensity of the moment of "Now". Listen to any background sounds even in the quietness. Did you succeed? Remember, just no thoughts for one minute. In Heaven, time does not exist. There is only the "Now". Time is purely a physical thing.... the revolution of the Earth, the hours in the day, the days in a year. We should learn to live more in the moment of the "Now" and appreciate every moment of your life as a gift from God................ even in the hardest of times.

Right, now as you sit quietly think about your most pressing problem at the moment. Quietly say a prayer to God, or think a prayer in your mind, and ask for help. Then, leave it at that...............you have passed your problem up to God. Within minutes, hours, or a day or so you may be surprised how suddenly you become aware of an answer to your problem. Alternatively, you may just feel better about yourself, and the problem will be something that you find the strength and wisdom to handle.

This "Sudden answer" is real help from your Guardian Angel. So how has the Angel communicated? Well, by helping you, the feeling of being helped, the intuition that you receive. Sensing Angels gives you greater certainty that there is life after death. This helps you personally handle grief from bereavement better. You can never get over bereavement, yet you can get through it. It helps you see that your own life is just part of an eternal process of the life of your soul. Your soul is the bit inside of you that you know as "I" or "Me".

Messages from Angels can help people with problems in their lives including problems of finances, relationships, stress, ill health, worry, insecurity, lacking in fulfilment. Angels can see situations surrounding people. Giving them messages that are of real help often astonishes people and helps them believe. This opens minds to show them that they can receive spiritual love, strength, wisdom and support. It is even possible to look at their future life-plan to get them back on course

As a person who can receive messages from the Angels, I find it easy to see some things in the future for a person that I am giving a reading. However, while these things I see are always good, positive things that a person would want, I realise that the same person might still be going through life difficulties, things going wrong in their life that seem terribly unfair.

When I see a person's future, images appear in my mind's eye. The mind's eye can also be called the "Third Eye". The images appear in a way that is familiar to all of us. For example, if I say "Visualise "Big Ben in London", even though you might have never been there, you will have seen photos or video of Big Ben, and an image might appear in your mind.

I am often given images of the future of things that are not familiar to me, but absolutely relate to the person I am reading. It could be a new home, a new car, or an image of a person whom they are yet to meet in a new friendship. It could be a place they might travel, a new job, or success in sport, or artistic achievement.

The images come into my mind easily as visions, but fortune tellers might use visual aids such as cards, a crystal ball, or even reading tea leaves!

Spiritual Energies in Nature

When out walking I often see flashes of light, especially in woodland and near streams, rivers and lakes. The Angels are constantly trying to maintain nature, and I see their light energies as they intensify when bring in healing to trees, plants, animals and birds. I can understand why folklore legends of fairies and other mythical creatures exist as some people may have seen the same flashes of light.

Spiritual Energy controls nature. Migrating birds "Know" where to go as they travel many thousands of miles because intelligent spiritual energies guide them. Homing pigeons are guided in the same way. Scientists believe that these birds are guided by the magnetic field, as used in a simple compass. The Earth's magnetic field only work North to South, not fully three hundred and sixty degrees, as would be necessary to use it for guidance.

CASE STUDIES

A reading, where an Angel brings messages from a loved one who has passed, can change a person's future

I gave Angel messages to a lady called Anne. I had never met her before, and she appeared to be aged in her early seventies. The only question I asked is for her name, and then I asked her to say nothing, except to confirm or otherwise the things I would describe.

I was immediately given a vision of a lady in spirit whom I

knew to be her mother. She was stood, as they usually do, to the left side of Anne. I described her mother's hair. It was grey, not coloured, and curly. This is where I am not very good at description because I don't know the names of different hairstyles. I told Anne my vision and I said, "It looks like her hair was nicely kept, and "Permed". Anne smiled for the first time and confirmed what I was seeing. "She is wearing a dark blue cardigan and black skirt". "That will be her, she often dressed exactly like that," said Anne.

Then my Angel suddenly gave me the name "Dorothy" spoken into my mind. "I have the name Dorothy" I said. Anne confirmed: "Yes, that was my mother's name".

My Angel Guide then gave me a vision in my Third Eye of her mother in bed, very sick, with Anne caring for her. I heard the words "Please thank her". I relayed the message to Anne that she had to care for her mother. I knew instantly that this had meant that Anne had to live with her mother towards the end of her mother's life. I said to Anne "I can see that you sacrificed a lot to live with your mother to care for her. She thanks you for that". Anne began to show emotional tears and was overwhelmed in a happy way to receive the message of thanks. I then saw a vision of a locket, holding a photo of her mother. I described the locket to Anne, and she pulled it out from where it was hidden behind her coat. It was exactly as described. I went on to give more detail that her mother communicated to me.

At the end of the reading Anne told me how she had previously held no beliefs in a life after death. She had felt insecure and cold inside following the recent death of her mother. Her life, her future, was changed for the better. She knew absolutely that no-one could have given her the information that came through the reading. She knew it was her mother. She would no longer carry the heavy weight of grief. She could move forward with her life feeling better.

Here is a case where a lady age around thirty years was able to see a brighter future following help from the Angels

Leanne came to see me. She seemed quite happy and bright. When I give a reading my first thought is "Do they want Angel messages from a love-one who has passed, or do they want messages concerning their life issues?" I never ask them this question. My Angel Guide usually points me in the right direction quite rapidly.

In this case it was a need for guidance concerning life issues. I saw that she was no longer in a relationship with a partner, and that she had two young children. As I began to tell her, Leanne confirmed that as correct. Suddenly I saw a vision of her being mentally and physically abused and attacked by her ex-partner, and that this had happened on a regular basis. This was quite a dramatic vision, and as I relayed and described this to her, she confirmed that this was exactly how her relationship had been. She had escaped her relationship in fear of her life.

"It isn't over yet" is what I told her. "Your ex-partner is still making threats to personally harm you". That is correct" she said. "I have a Court Injunction that states he cannot come near my house, but he is so violent that it sometimes doesn't stop him trying to get to me. I need to move home, live somewhere that he can't find me"

I then realised that the Angels were giving me visions of the future for her. I saw a new man in her life. A very caring person. I described him in detail starting with his hairstyle and hair colour, the shape of his face, his stature, and the clothes he might typically wear. Leanne had a look of amazement as she opened-up a photo on her phone. "Is this him?" she asked. The photo was exactly the image I could see in my vision. She was astonished at my description of this new man and felt she might start to trust this new relationship that she had found. I then told her that he had been in a relationship that had failed, and that he had one child, a daughter, with shared custody with his ex. She confirmed this.

I concluded by describing a vision of her spending her future life with him, much happier, and able to move away from her current location. I gave her a warning that this new man could be prone to being quiet and moody after finishing work, and that he is quite serious in his work as a baker. Leanne laughed and said that she could cope with that.

At the end, she expressed amazement at how I could have known the information that I had given her. She felt that her fear and reluctance to move on with her life could now be worked through, and that she could gradually, step by step, move forward in her new relationship.

CHAPTER SIX

Sensing Angels

Learning how to sense Angels is important. It is achieved as part of our personal spiritual development. We don't need to sense Angels all of the time.

I can't sense Angels when I am at work or watching television or doing anything that occupies my mind. In the 21st century most of us are occupying our minds with work, entertainment, social media, and countless other thoughts. Many people stay awake at night worrying about things. The Angels can only be sensed when our mind is quiet. In order to sense Angels for yourself the first thing to do is allow yourself some quiet time. You do not necessarily need to spend time in a quiet room. You could be out walking on a safe, quiet path, away from traffic.

Angels are from Heaven, but if we try too hard to sense spiritual energies, we might feel uncomfortable because we might also sense negative energies.

We need to say a prayer, in our mind to the God, or the Highest loving Source in whom you believe. Pray for the ability to sense Angels from Heaven. Prayers can be heard because in Heaven we speak to each other using our thoughts. It is important to pray for protection from evil, negative energies. In our prayers ask to be guided by Heaven, given strength by Heaven, and be totally protected from negative energies that might seek to hurt ourselves or our families.

We should try to sense Angels in different settings. In a quiet room can you sense a gently, loving someone with you?

Whilst out walking in woodland can you sense the unseen spiritual energy of the trees as if they are looked after by an Angel? I have witnessed Angels in woodland settings, especially near a stream, as flashes of light. This happens when they bring healing to nature and the healing energies of the Angels intensify. Often, when I see these flashes of light, I think that such visions could account for people witnessing fairies and other mythical creatures. Of course, I always ask questions when I see an Angel, and the usual explanation when I see them in nature is to be shown the tree, flower, or plant that the Angels are healing. This can also be a rabbit, bird, or other wildlife. Often the healing is for an entire area of forest or vegetation.

Many people feel a sense of exhilaration and well-being when walking in the countryside. At times we may experience a scenic view and our spiritual senses seem heightened in awareness. With an understanding of Angels who are close to us, but often unseen, we can sense them intensely when we are experiencing heightened spiritual awareness.

Sensing Angels through our intuitive feelings

Have you ever felt that you shouldn't have gone somewhere, and you ignored the feeling? Then something bad happened?

The following is a true account: A lady refused to board a plane to fly on holiday with her husband. They had flown many times before and she wasn't afraid of flying. She had a strong intuitive feeling that something bad was going to happen to the flight. They missed their flight and cancelled their holiday. They heard nothing on the news afterwards, and her husband wasn't happy that their holiday was cancelled. However, they spoke to friends who had taken the same flight. There had been confusion concerning what was happening to the flight amongst passengers. They had experienced severe weather, engine problems, and had to make an emergency landing. Fortunately, no-one was hurt, but it had been a terrifying experience for those on board.

Have you ever met someone you knew whilst in a distant place? Sometimes the Angels steer the timelines of our lives to converge in physical places, perhaps resulting in a meeting that we find helpful to our current life situation.

Have you ever experienced coincidences, the odds of which are happening can be remote? I won't give examples of coincidences. Some are genuine happenings that happen by chance. It is always worth thinking about every coincidence to see if your Guardian Angel is trying to tell you something.

Sensing help from Angels – "Sudden Knowingness"
Have you ever experienced moments of "Sudden Knowingness"? You might have been wrestling with a problem for some time and then suddenly, as if from nowhere you know what to do.
You might have been in communication with someone and suddenly feel quite strongly that they are mistaken or not telling the truth.
You are planning to travel somewhere and then suddenly get a strong feeling that you will experience some difficulties.
Our Guardian Angels try to guide us. They can often see a way forward through challenges and problems. They communicate their guidance instantly into our mind so effectively that we experience these moments of "Sudden Knowingness". It is always good to trust these intuitive messages. We can learn to trust these as we strengthen our knowledge concerning the Angels.

A Real-Life Example of Sudden Knowingness.
A friend of mine was quite distraught because one of her cats had gone missing. I realised that she lived on a street with many houses around but directed her to the end house where I felt her

cat was somehow trapped.

She asked at all the houses, including the end house, and no-one had seen her cat. Several days later her cat was still missing. As a person, just me, I didn't know what to say. Suddenly, my Guardian Angel gave me a vision. I described to her what I saw "Go back to the end house and insist on looking in the rear garden for a side door that leads into a garage. Insist that you look inside. You will not see your cat because he is trapped behind some furniture. He is very weak, but still alive." My friend did exactly as I said. A lady who lives at the end house insisted that she had searched for my friend's cat and that it wasn't there. However, my friend insisted she look in the garage. She saw furniture stored in there but could not see her cat. She then shouted the cat's name, and a feint "Meow" came from behind the furniture. Some furniture had to be partly dismantled to release her cat. He was very weak, but fortunately has now fully recovered to good health.

How do we Speak to each other in Heaven?

My spiritual research concerning the subject of how we communicate with each other in Heaven led me to a conclusion that this is one of the most important principles to learn and understand in how to sense our Guardian Angels.

In Heaven, although we still retain our individuality, we also realise that we are spiritually connected with each other, with the Angels, and with everyone. We sense a Oneness that is hard to describe.

Communication in Heaven can be with the words of the language that we learnt whilst in physical life. However, we were born out of Heaven as a baby without language skills, so how did we communicate before birth? The answer is that communication in Heaven is by projecting our feelings and thoughts. This is the same as the "Instant Knowingness" that I describe as one of the ways our Guardian Angels communicate with us.

In our life as a human being, some people have experiences of "Telepathy". I believe that this isn't a trick of the human brain, but genuinely a moment of spiritual connection with someone else that enables a transfer of thoughts or projection of feelings. Our thoughts and feelings that we project as a human being are capable of being picked up by Heaven, and by our Guardian Angel. We shouldn't worry about our quiet inner thoughts and feelings because the Angels and Heaven cannot listen to them. Although we might project negative, frustrated, angry thoughts sometimes, it is our actions, not our thoughts, that Heaven sees.

How do we project our thoughts?

In Heaven we project our thoughts and feelings to communicate with other people who have physically died and are now in Heaven nearby. Our Guardian Angel will still be with us, and we will communicate by projecting thoughts and feelings.

When we are born as a baby, we immediately lose the ability to project our thoughts. We have to learn language, but whilst we are learning we are given the instinctive ability to cry when we are hungry, tired, or suffering discomfort. We soon develop an ability to laugh when we are happy.

Once we have learnt how to use language and mathematical skills then these become the primary ways that we project our thoughts. Language can also be expressed by signs made with the hand and face for those with hearing impairment. Language is a projection of some of our thoughts. We need to use the correct words and make the communication more effective using the tone of our voice and perhaps physical expressions. We can show these expressions with our face, our hands, and the stance we take. Do we frown or express anger as we speak loudly, or do we smile and speak gently? Do we get physically closer to someone, or move slightly away? How do we use our hands and arms? Are we pointing at someone, or keeping our hands relaxed?

So, in Heaven we can project our thoughts and feelings instantly and completely. Whilst in physical life as a human being we learn how to project our thoughts through language, tone of voice and body expressions, although this is a slower process than "Instant Knowingness".

Human beings have always sought ever more clever and instant ways to communicate out thoughts, feelings and messages. It cannot be underestimated how important the development of the written word was as a skill that changed our world forever. The ability to write was developed several thousand years ago and it was seen as a miracle. Some learned people in higher developed societies were now able to write their communication in words that could be read exactly word for word, as a story being retold time after time. People in different areas, countries and periods of time could read the same communication of thoughts that the writer put down on stone, paper or parchment. In the early periods of writing only a few people had the opportunity to learn the skills of writing and reading. The countless millions of others who could only hear words been read must have been left with feelings of wonder and awe. Many religions have been founded by the written Word as being itself a miracle of communication. The miracle of the written Word helped people who listened to accept what the written Word was telling them.

Humanity continues to seek better and more rapid means of communication. Perhaps it is the inner memories of Heaven, where communication is instant, that drives humanity on this quest. The internet and world wide web, phone technology, emails, television and social media have transformed communication throughout the world and into our personal lives.

Angels are spiritual beings from Heaven, and are a link between us, and Heaven. They still communicate by projection of thoughts and feelings to give us "Instant Knowingness". I hope that humanity can learn to recognise that we cannot always expect words and language messages from Heaven, although the Angels do sometimes communicate with us using words and language.

We need to start to "Sense" the "Projection of Thoughts" messages from the Angels and we can do this by understanding the difference between how Heaven communicates, and how people in life communicate.

Human beings can comminate some of their feelings by projecting them as we do in Heaven. Examples of these are strong feelings of love or anger. This is not as straightforward or easy as it is in Heaven. We can project our feelings of love to someone, and they might pick up these feelings without the need for words. However, the person to whom you project your feeling of love might be blocking you or shielding themselves from sensing any feelings being projected by anyone at them. Some people do this instinctively because it also helps protect them from feelings of anger that are around.

Prayer Works

Having explained how we, and the Angels communicate in Heaven, it might be easier to understand that Prayer is a way of projecting our thoughts and feelings. Our prayers are heard, even if they are projected silently from our mind. To project them is easy, and simply means that we should think of ourselves as talking to someone. That someone being God.

Our prayers, even silent in our minds, are projected thoughts that can be heard by Heaven. We should always pray to the Highest Authority in Heaven whom we believe. I believe in God, so the Highest Authority in my belief is God.

The Angels work in the purpose of Heaven, and although we can thank the Angels, we should always pray to God, and give thanks to God. If our prayer is said with goodness in our soul, then it will be responded to with powerful, positive help from Heaven through the Angels.

As I understand, God doesn't need thanking. However, the process of thanking God, and words of worship help our personal spiritual growth. The reason? Throughout history many, many people have ruled countries, or have been in control of companies, organisations and people and have shown little empathy because they behave as though they themselves are some kind of god.

Whenever we feel our problems are too much for us, or we need healing for ourselves or someone we know, say a prayer to God. The Angels will try to help. I say an inner prayer in my mind many times every day. The Angels respond by helping me through life problems, help to protect me from negative energies, and bring healing and calm. I also pray for life fulfilment and a way forward into the future. I am constantly praying for the world, and others around.

Angels Come into our Dreams

An important way in which Angels communicate with us is through dreams.

I have received many accounts from people who tell me that a loved one who has passed came through to them in their dreams. I always say to them "If the dream felt as though it was an intense experience, and that it was "Real" then your loved one came through". This is a form of clairvoyance that many people experience, and it is helped by the Angels.

I remember one of many instances when I was a Methodist preacher, visiting a friend whose husband had recently died. Firstly, I could see her husband stood with her in spirit, anxious to give her a message. As a Christian preacher at the time I couldn't tell her because mediumship is condemned by Christianity. However, I encouraged her to talk to me and she decribed her dream that she had the previous night. She had a very real experience of walking along a beach, hand-in-hand with her husband. She kept emphasising how real the dream experience was, and her being truly convinced that her husband had really been there for her. I did tell her that I believed her, and that it was a very real experience of reuniting with him.

Of course, many dreams are unpleasant nightmares. I believe that our brain creates dreams to entertain our soul as our body sleeps. When we are going through times of stress and worry our brain presents us with unpleasant dreams with a distorted and mixed up picture of our real life situations. Why does the brain do this? Perhaps it is a survival mechanism to keep our problems at the front of our mind so that we can quickly face them again when we awake.

Sometimes a loved one may try to get into our dreams when we are going through problems in our waking life. The brain will distort the experience of reuniting with the spirit of the loved one. This can turn what should be a beautiful dream into a mixed up dream of pleasant and unpleasant emotions that we cannot make sense of.

CHAPTER SEVEN

Premonitions

I have now experienced many instances where the Angels have given me visions and messages from Heaven concerning the future. This could be a vision of a future for a person I am helping with an Angel Messages reading, or a premonition concerning a future local, national, or world event. Because everything I do and see is then linked back to my logical research, I believe that it is the correct moment in time to explain this to a wider audience. I believe that the knowledge could make the world a better place as more people seek to learn the enlightenment that can be revealed through this knowledge. The gifts of Sensing Angels and the ability to receive premonitions are, absolutely, spiritual skills. They are only possible if we can accept that the Spiritual Realm of Heaven is another dimension. It is the familiar home where our soul came from, and where we will return after our physical life on Earth. Until now religious beliefs have made claim to our understanding of the Spiritual Realm. I will not criticise religions for they offer much truth, despite disagreement with one another. However, we do not have to be religious to Sense Angels. Heaven loves us all unconditionally.

Have you ever experienced a premonition? If so, you might not have known how to handle it, or whether to take it seriously. Our modern, materialistic societies don't teach us how to handle premonitions because they are not taken seriously in mainstream belief.

Premonitions concerning happenings in the world

Unlike reading a person's future, premonitions are given to me unannounced, and without prior thoughts of the events in the premonition given to me.

Premonitions work for me in two ways:

1) If a person I am in contact with is to travel somewhere, I might receive a premonition of any serious weather, natural catastrophe, or other personal danger. I also experience such premonitions for myself.

2) I am constantly experiencing premonitions of global events. I was told by my Angel Guide that something big would affect the entire world in 2020. The "Something Big" turned out to be the COVID-19 Pandemic. Climate Change, and the consequences to nature, and our planet is on the minds of many people, and the subject of many of my premonitions.

The following examples are all true accounts of premonitions that came true:

Tsunami

I was given a vision of the Boxing Day Tsunami of December 2004. The vision was given to me six months earlier. I warned a family member not to travel to a beach resort in Thailand because of my visions of a huge wall of water from the sea overwhelming the coastline and going inland. I didn't know what a Tsunami was, but just saw a huge wall of water. My family member listened to the warning that our Guardian Angels had given and said she would think twice about her planned travel to that area. She and her husband had spent months training to be diving instructors and were to work for a year as diving instructors for tourists at a holiday beach resort in Thailand. Naturally, they were annoyed at my warnings. Fortunately, for several other reasons they cancelled their plans. Her friends, husband and wife plus a son aged four, had made the same plans, and did journey there. When the Tsunami hit, the man was diving underwater, and was swept four miles down the coast, but was uninjured. The woman saved herself and her son by running inland, and she held her son above her head as the water reached shoulder height. Fortunately, they were not injured.

I receive premonitions of danger for myself when I travel. The following true account is just one example.

Bus on fire

It was around 5.30 pm one Spring evening in May 2018, I had to travel home from work by bus because my car was in a garage for repairs. The journey was twelve miles across country from Driffield to Bridlington, Yorkshire. It was a double decker bus, and I was seated downstairs on the left side. I had boarded the bus in Driffield and at the final stop before leaving Driffield I suddenly saw flames rising upwards at the outside of the window alongside of me. Yet, passengers were getting on the bus, obviously not seeing the flames. The flames appeared like those in a cartoon, in full colour orange, yet is if they were drawn by an artist. The vision disappeared as quickly as it came. I didn't know what to do, so I continued my bus journey. Six miles along the road in open countryside the bus suddenly stopped. The engine at the rear had suddenly blown up, with steam and oil everywhere, but no flames. Fortunately, no-one was hurt. I reflected later that I hadn't heeded the warning that my Guardian Angel gave me.

Messages I hear as a voice

I might occasionally hear a spiritual voice from my Guardian Angel when trying to help someone is emotionally stressed.

The voice is always the same, giving me a clear message, but with no emotional expression.

The messages always seem to communicate a healing and happy

outcome within four weeks, or in one month. The predicted outcome is almost unbelievable at the time.

Here is a real-life example:

Again, this true account concerns a family member. It was Easter 2019 when I spent several hours trying to console a family member whose fiancée had just left him. They had been in a relationship for seven years, yet she had refused to share a home with him. The relationship seemed to be finished with phone contact and social media contact blocked. I didn't move into psychic mode, and, as most people, I began to feel drained of energy as I tried for several hours to help him feel better, but without success.

I needed a break so went to the bathroom. Suddenly the voice I hear spiritually, speaking with no emotion into my mind said: "She will be back in his life in a full relationship and sharing a home in one month". I went back to join my family member, who was suffering severe depression. How could I tell him about the message? I plucked up the courage and told him. He knows my psychic gift and believes me. He became less depressed, and more positive than he had been all day. One month to the exact day later it transpired that not only were they back together, but she moved in to share a home with him.

I always trust that inner voice. It is the voice of my Guardian Angel, and the Angels can see our future.

The following is a further true account of how some may receive premonitions:

I was giving an Angel messages reading to an elderly lady at her home in the city of Hull. My Angel brought through a vision and messages concerning her father who had been a fisherman on a Hull trawler during his working life. I then brought through a picture of a trawler sinking with loss of life of all those on board. The lady looked astonished and briefly confirmed the facts, but I asked her not to say anything further.

The Angels then showed me a vision of how her father had refused to board ship one day. He had felt intuitively that something bad was going to happen to the trawler that he worked on. He went home and the trawler set sail without him, never to be return home again due to severe weather.

The lady confirmed everything as true that her deceased father via the Angels had just told me. She then went on to say that he had lived a healthy and full life before he died of natural causes aged in his eighties.

This account shows clearly how many people can receive intuitive feelings. My research show that these are given to us by our Guardian Angels. Some people listen to these feelings and act on them, but many people don't. In this book I explain how important it is for all of us to start to believe in our intuitive feelings and be guided by them throughout life. This is extremely important in helping us to Sense Angels.

CHAPTER EIGHT

How Angels Communicate with us

Angels communicate into our thoughts so completely that we may just take them as being our own thoughts. We have free will. Our inner voice might not even be a voice because it is a series of thoughts that try to warn us and guide us. We constantly create our own thoughts, but the inner voice is different in that the thought, and ideas suddenly come from nowhere. I best describe this as a sudden "knowingness".

With free will, we can choose to ignore our inner voice. If we do this frequently enough then we lose our close relationship with our Guardian. We may then become reckless in our actions, and inconsiderate, lacking in empathy for other people, and for animals, nature and the environment.

We may have spiritual callings such as charity work, concern for animals, concern for nature, concern for the planet. When we balance our free will thoughts with our inner voice from our Guardian then our spiritual callings will bear fruit. We can and do generate our own love for others, and we have our own skills and abilities.

Guardian Angels are a part of our conscience. Our conscience is within our inner self and may whisper to us that something we have done, or are considering doing may hurt someone, or hurt an animal, or hurt nature.

Some people become so self-centred that they never listen to their Guardian Angel.

In such cases their Guardian is unable to give thought into the minds of these people that act as their conscience. Eventually this cutting off from their Guardian is so total that they no longer hear the inner voice. Their Guardian cannot get through to them. Such people might seem to be civilised and confine their self-centred actions to walking over others legally in business, career, or relationships. They, and others can, and do hurt people physically or mentally without feeling guilty.

Negative, earthbound spirits of evil energies cannot get inside anyone who has still a connection with their Guardian Angel. Our Guardians protect us from negative energies. The earth plane does have a lot of negative energy. Spirits who are evil can still be bound to the earth plane and seek opportunities to target individuals who have torn away from their Guardian. Negative, evil spirits can then try to communicate directly into their thoughts. If such a person has a dark character, it is easy for the evil spirit to stoke their fire of self-centred purpose to cause harm. This type of person goes out and does harm to others and has no conscience concerning harming animals and nature.

Our Guardians work through our intuition, giving sudden answers to problems, feelings inside about what to do. These seem to come from nowhere. An impossible overpowering problem can suddenly be answered by seeing what to do.

Spiritual Talents

Our Guardian Angels can almost become one with us, melding into our being, when we are using our spiritual talents to help others, help animals, help nature or work to help the environment. This "As one" feeling may produce a totality of our inner strength, determination, and spiritual powers to enable us to do the work.

I firmly believe that many scientific discoveries have been inspired inside the thoughts of our great scientists by their Guardians as part of some Higher Plan.

Our Guardian Angels can also work externally in helping these things around happen in a better way for you.

Angels can help us achieve that deep-down longing for fulfilment that most of us yearn. We all have different talents and ability, and our Guardians can help us make the most of what we have got.

The most successful people achieve their ambitions and personal goals through being totally focused. They have tunnel vision and imagine where they want to be and what they want to achieve. If their vision is good, and will cause no hurt or harm, then they will be helped by listening closely to the inner voice from their Guardian Angel. People are mostly unaware that their own thoughts and visions can be enhanced by their Guardian, who may feed them ideas, inspiration, motivation and positive energy along the way.

Yes, our Guardians feed us many differing kinds of positive spiritual Energy!

Guardian Angels are Beings of Unconditional Love from the Spiritual Realm of Heaven and will never put thoughts in people's minds that will cause hurt or harm in any way.

OUR GUARDIAN ANGELS CHANNEL HEALING TO US

Amazing reports of significant healing benefits have been received from people who have received healing from the Heaven via the Angels

Healing can be towards a quicker recovery from illness, to ease the pain of stress or bereavement, or to ease depression.
Healing can be to our lives, to provide a happier and brighter future and personal fulfilment through greater success in whatever we do.

You may think "I don't often need healing, for I am generally in good health".
Alternatively, you may think "I don't have a Guardian Angel healing me, for I am always unwell".
Our Guardian Angels constantly bring healing to us
Our human body is frail in this harsh world we live in. It is a miracle that we can survive with such a fragile body, constantly at risk from injury and accident, and constantly exposed to germs that cause illness.
Many people damage their health through bad diet, smoking, drinking alcohol, lack of exercise. Our Guardian Angels are constantly working to help us when our free will actions are

harming our bodies

That miracle is the constant work by our Guardian Angels, healing, protecting, guiding us away from danger, and trying to keep our immune systems, and other bodily defences at optimum efficiency.

LIFE ENERGIES

Our Guardian Angels channel Healing Life Energies into us.

Life Energies can be a shade of purple, which is pure healing energy, Springtime light green for renewing body cells, and Golden for renewing Life Energy, plus many other shades of the colour spectrum.

Angels are also constantly at work channeling life energies in nature to forests, flowers, animals, and all of life. Although I sense Angels all of the time, I only see them when they intensify their energies to bring-in healing to people or to nature. The following photo is a visual image of an Angel channeling healing energies to trees in woodlands, East Yorkshire, England.

The following is a true account of an Angel channeling healing energies to a person:

A was giving a lady an Angel messages reading, and the Angels gave me some meaningful messages from her grandma, who had raised her throughout childhood, and had been a loving mother because her real mother had left the family for another relationship. Towards the end of the reading, I was given a message that she was in severe pain with her left knee. She confirmed what I said and told me that she was to have a knee operation, to fit a replacement knee, the next day. I asked her if she would like some spiritual healing and she agreed.

When I channel Angel healing, it is non-contact. I hold my hand a few centimetres away from a person's forehead and talk though what happens. I immediately saw several healing Angels come in close. One Angel projected a blue energy to bring pain relief and ease the inflammation around her knee area. Another brought in a Springtime green energy to help renewal of the damaged cells in her muscles and tendons. A beautiful purple energy came in to bring powerful healing to her. I could see the Angels shimmering with the colour of the Life Energies they channelled.

The lady became very relaxed and started to feel well as the pain disappeared.

I saw the lady a few weeks later. She was walking without pain, and excited to tell me that the knee replacement operation had gone exceptionally well, and she had made a recovery much quicker than her surgeon had expected. She commented that she was convinced that this was due to the powerful benefit of the healing she had received from the Angels.

Another true account

I gave an Angel messages reading to a young woman who was pregnant, but her personal health was damaged by an extremely bad "Junk Food" diet, smoking, drinking alcohol etc. Her baby was subsequently born perfect. I am not a medical person but know enough about the human body to realise that our cells need the correct nutrition, trace elements, proteins, that are the building blocks of life. I am certain many of you reading this will have known a mother with similar lifestyle, although I realise that babies can be born with health problems from mothers who don't take care of their personal health.

I asked my Guardian Angel: "How can the baby have such perfection?"
My Guardian replied: "Through invisible Life Energy the Healing Angels can channel into a baby in the womb the building blocks of Life that people might truly believe can only come from nutrients in food, or from the mother"

Intuition

Our Guardian Angels work through our intuition, giving sudden answers to problems, and feelings inside about what to do. These seem to come from nowhere. An impossible overpowering problem can be answered by suddenly seeing what needs to be done.
Angels communicate into our thoughts so completely that we just take them as being our own thoughts.

Conscience

Our Guardian Angels work through our conscience so strongly that my research indicates our conscience may be up to 100% our Guardian Angel.
As human beings we all have the gift of Free Will. It seems that our Guardian Angels cannot prevent us from making our Free Will decisions in everyday life. What they can and do is to put feelings into our minds that we commonly describe as our "Conscience". These feelings are like an inner voice, urging us not to do something

that may hurt others.

Many of our actions in life impact directly on others. If our actions in some way cause hurt to others, either emotionally, psychologically, or physically then our conscience should make us aware of this. We may question our conscience and say: "Well, I know a person, or other people may not like what I intend to do, but it is for "Good" in the long-term."

Alternatively, we may just go-ahead and do things which hurt others in some way, and our actions are for our own self-centred needs and satisfaction.

Our conscience should always tell us if we are doing something spiritually wrong.

Some people are so self-centred that they always ignore their conscience. Eventually they lose their conscience completely. Their Guardian Angel cannot get through.

Something new starts to happen. When a Guardian Angel stands back because someone is totally self-centred and is going through life hurting others, then it leaves a spiritual void. The void is caused because the Guardian Angel has had to stand back, cannot get through and cannot protect the individual from negative, evil energies.

Negative energies are always around waiting on the earth plane, waiting for an opportunity to get into someone who is no longer protected by their Guardian Angel.

Once negative energy starts to influence a person then their evil actions towards others become more intense and more frequent.

Spiritual Gifts

We all have some Spiritual Gift. It is better not to envy or be jealous about someone else's spiritual gift, but to try to identify our gift, and make the most of it.

We may have spiritual gifts such as a need to help others,

concern for animals, concern for nature, concern for the planet. When we balance our free will thoughts with our inner voice from our Guardian then our spiritual gifts will bear fruit. We can and do generate our own love for others, and we have our own skills and abilities.

People who have an inner driving force that helps others, or helps nature, or helps the environment can be classed as having a spiritual gift.

Guardian Angels help us when
we work to help others

Our Guardian Angel will help us with our work, and at times almost become one with us in terms of spiritual energy and purpose. At such times we will care less about ourselves, other than keeping ourselves healthy, and be almost totally dedicated to the purpose of helping others.

Problems and Guidance

Angels communicate into our thoughts so completely that we just take them as being our own thoughts.

We have free will. Our inner voice is not even a voice but thoughts that warn us, guide us. Don't get me wrong, we constantly create our own thoughts. The inner voice is different in that the thought, and ideas suddenly come from nowhere. I best describe this as a sudden "knowingness".

With Free Will we can choose to ignore our inner voice. If we do this frequently enough then we lose our close relationship with our Guardian. We may then become reckless in our actions, and inconsiderate, lacking in empathy for other people for animals, nature and the environment.

Real Life Examples of how our Guardian Angels Guide us

Self: "I want to earn a lot of money. I will earn money by becoming a pop star or successful actor"
Guardian: "These are not your talents. Don't try to be something you haven't the talent for."
Focus on what you feel from your Guardian you can do, try hard, and be a success!
Self: "I am out shopping but don't know where to go for a gift for my family member/ friend. I am getting stressed and tired."
Guardian: "Just blank your thoughts, slow down. You will suddenly know which shop to go into and be drawn to a suitable gift." This is your Guardian at work!

A "Calling"

Ever wondered why some people are so determined to do something to help others? Why some people are determined to work helping animals, nature, or the environment?
I believe that many people are given a "Calling". This is a gift from Heaven to do a particular task. The task is part of a Divine Plan to make sure that every aspect of life has people interested in caring and working to cherish, protect, repair and bring healing.

Our Guardian Angels know this Divine Plan and work to help those with a Calling to help them fulfil their inner driving force to care for other people, or care for animals, nature, and planet Earth.
Our Guardian Angels Can Give Us Special Help.

At times we may need special help in life.

For ourselves we may need special healing in times of health crises.

We may need extra help through difficult situations.

For others we may wish for urgent healing when seriously ill or injured. For others we may wish for their lives to be urgently improved from bad situations.

How Can We Ask for Special Help?

We ask for Special Help through Prayer. Yes, prayer either in our thoughts, or out loud. Prayer alone, or in unison and harmony with others.

Our thoughts and prayers are heard in Heaven because Heaven is a place of pure thought.

How do we Pray?

We should never pray to our Guardian Angels. They work in the purpose of God, and on the instructions of God.

We should always pray to God. Pray upwards to the Highest Spiritual Authority, to God, and the powerful, loving actions needed to answer our prayer will be passed back down to our Guardian Angels.

ANGELS HELP US TOWARDS OUR DREAMS OF FUTURE ACHIEVEMENT

Firstly: What is your vision of what you want for the future? Are such dreams positive and good?

Secondly: What talents and abilities do you have? What talents and abilities don't you have?

Thirdly: You can fight through disability. You can fight through being in the wrong part of society. You can fight through lack of academic ability or achievement. You can fight through having no start-up money.

Fourthly: You will find it harder in a society that suppresses people. Your dreams must be realistic within the society you live. Our Guardians work through our dreams. Not all the time. When a dream seems REAL then it will be real.

Our Guardian Angels are of the Spiritual Realm and can link our soul to Heaven whilst we are in dream state. This might be to link to loved ones who have passed. I have heard many people tell me how they experienced dreams that seemed like real life with their husband/wife/parents who had passed.

Dreams frequently give us mixed visions of our life events that are difficult to interpret. Our physical brain replays current life experiences, and these can be mixed with spiritual visions from our Guardians.

Dreams are taken seriously by many people.

FREE WILL: THE MOST DIFFICULT PART OF OUR PERSON

Angels stand back when our Free Will is driven by self-centred behaviour that will hurt others.

We are all given a life for an important purpose. That purpose is to spiritually grow.

Our life on Earth as human beings is a transient experience.

We are in Heaven before we are born, and we return to Heaven at the end of physical life.

We are given life to experience being human. Interaction with others in our relationships with people is a massive part of that experience. We are given life for learning, for adventure, for the physical experiences of walking, running free, sport, and competition.

We seek to find love again, as we experienced in Heaven, where love is the air that we breathe. We may find love in our mother's arms as a baby. We seek love in our relationships as we grow older. Sometimes such love can be confusing because it is tainted by desire.

The true unconditional love from Heaven is still with us through our Guardian Angel. If we recognise our Guardian Angel as close to us, then we may feel that love with us most of the time. If we choose by our Free Will to distance ourselves from our Guardian Angel, then we may feel cold and isolated inside.

Free Will is given to us because as spiritual beings we are respected by Heaven.

We can choose to do what we want in life, but often our Free Will urges may knock us off the path of our Life Plan. Things go wrong and we wonder why.

The most destructive parts of Free Will become apparent when we choose to ignore our Guardian Angel. Many of the populations of the world are not even aware of their Guardian Angels, so Free Will choices are made without this high level of awareness. Often, we find people acting in a self-centred way, not caring too much if they hurt others emotionally, psychologically, or physically.

Through their Free Will many people inadvertently or deliberately go against all the ways their Guardian Angels try to Guide them. These ways are through a person's conscience, intuition, and caring thoughts. On far too many occasions Guardian Angels are forced to stand back, for such is the gift of Free Will that we are allowed to prioritise the decisions we make for ourselves, even when we cause harm.

Negative energy is not far away in all our lives. The world is constantly generating all kinds of spiritual energy from the vast number of spirits in the form of living people that are currently in life.

Love is the strongest, most powerful energy of all, constantly battling against the negative, evil energies in our physical universe. If people, through their Free Will, choose to act in a self-centred way that may hurt other people, or hurts nature or the environment in a big way then their Guardian Angel cannot get through. The tragedy is that negative entities might then see an opportunity to get through into the minds of these people. This makes their self-centred behaviour move in the direction of evil. This is a big subject!

I can describe to people I read through the visions Angels give me of their personal future, but with the ability to help them change their future to be happy and fulfilling. This is an important factor because we all could change our futures if we learn to recognise and accept spiritual guidance that can be available for us every minute of every day.

Guardian Angels are working through many, many people via their intuition, to give them a "Calling" to help during a pandemic, and longer-term to avert the more serious consequences of Climate Change. That is why some people seem extremely dedicated to this work.

We need to educate the world concerning the spiritual guidance that can be sought concerning real ways and actions to avoid the serious consequences of climate change.

CHAPTER NINE

Angel Visions

Angels can give us Visions

As an example of the Angels giving me visions, the following is a true account of a reading that involved seeing the future for a lady. Without her telling me anything beforehand, I discovered in the reading that her family were deeply troubled by what had happened to their son. During the reading I saw two outcomes for their son, one good, and one not so good, so I focussed on the good path, and the future changed as I spoke to become the better outcome.

The lady sitting in front of me screamed. Her scream shook the house and surely neighbours would come running in to see what had happened. I was a stranger who had been sat facing this lady across a kitchen table for no more than five minutes. Her scream shook me with an unexpected shudder of sudden stress because I am not the kind of guy who does anything to make women scream. I am a clairvoyant and she had booked me to visit her home to give her a reading. This lady was aged around 40 years and was obviously taking no care of her appearance with greasy hair all over the place, and scruffy clothes. She seemed depressed as she welcomed me into her house and sat me down.

My first words, from a vision given by my Angel Guide ,were simply "It's about Justice – or rather an injustice – your son is in prison for an offence he didn't commit" That is when she screamed. I had imagined some heavy-weight fighter of a husband appearing and throwing me out, but fortunately she had kicked him out of the house for a few hours for privacy during the reading. My Angel Guide had given me a vision of her son in prison accompanied by a message that he was innocent and would soon be freed. What I told her was correct, but then I went on to tell her that her son's prison sentence would be overturned, and he would be a free man within four weeks. Her scream was of surprise at how I could possibly know all of this. I spent another hour with her, bringing-in some quite clear messages from her deceased mother. She calmed down very quickly and became more optimistic and much happier over that hour, and the messages from her mum appeared to be of great meaning. I left her with good wishes, inside my mind saying a quiet prayer for her and her son.

This was in the city of Hull, which I only visit several times a year, and I never go to the public houses there. However, about a month later I did call into a Hull public bar with some friends, but in a different area of the city. Hull is a big place. Within minutes an attractive lady came running up to me and gave me a big hug saying: "It's him… it's him…". I couldn't help but notice a rather tough looking partner behind her looking quite angry at her behaviour. "It's ok," she told him. "This is the clairvoyant". The partner changed his mood, put a smile on his face and shook my hand. "Our son is no longer in prison, everything you said came true". The fact that their son was now free was good news, but the added miracle for me was the transformation of this lady. She had taken on a new zest for living, pulled herself out of depression, and acquired a new interest in taking care of herself. She had given herself a makeover with her hair and dress, with such a dramatic improvement that I hadn't recognised her immediately. This was the miracle of what clairvoyance can offer. I have witnessed this miracle many times as people take their lives off "hold" and start living again. My friends in the pub had been staring-on in amazement. I didn't openly discuss my work in giving people messages via the Angels. One of my hobbies was singing, and we had just done a concert, so my fellow singers in the pub knew nothing about me sensing Angels. I just tried to shoulder-off what had happened in a joking way.

Visions of Angels

Angels are reported to have been seen by human beings in different countries, different cultures, and across time. When an Angel appears it is usually a rare occurrence and to bring a profound message.

Experiencing visions of Angels in our everyday lives is not something that happens to most people.

I have discovered that we need to develop a clairvoyant ability as a starting point in learning to see Angels. Of course, this is easier said than done. However, the first step in seeing an Angel is to "Sense" through our intuitive feelings that an Angel is nearby. An Angel that might become visible.

How do I see Angels?

Guardian Angels appear without wings. Higher Angels appear with what seems like wings. The wings are shown because that is what we expect when we see an Angel. In their true soul form in Heaven they have a radiance.

Guardian Angels try not to be seen

When I give an Angel Messages reading I am often given

visions of a person in Heaven and visions of places that are meaningful to those who are with me. Guardian Angels bring these messages, and yet they often stand aside so that I only see the subject of the messages and not the Angel.

When I do see a Guardian Angel, the vision is often without wings and with the appearance of a male or female human being, usually wearing flowing robes and radiating light.

Angels can be present and visible in places where events occurred that triggered strong emotions.

When I see other Angels and Archangels they appear with wings. I visited Whitby Abbey in North Yorkshire, England and saw several monks in spirit plus much more. The Abbey is actually the ruins of a 13th century Church of the Benedictine Abbey built on the site. The original monastery was founded by St. Hilda in the seventh century. I sudddenly saw a vision of a beautiful Angel hovering in front of one area of ruins. Tears of emotion started to fill my eyes but I didn't know why. I asked a guide if there was any special history concerning the area of ruins where the Angel vision occurred. He replied "The Germans targeted shells at the Abbey, firing from the guns of their battle cruisers during World War One, and that is the area that was hit and damaged". That explanation helped me understand the emotions I was feeling. The Angel appeared with wings and was as tall as the ruins, radiating energy and light. I was given just one word by the Angel: "Protecting".

I later researched that on the morning of December 16th 1914, two German battlecruisers, the Derfflinger and the Von der Tann came close to shore at Scarborough, firing shells at Scarborough Castle, the Grand Hotel, and three Churches. There were many casualties. The battlecruisers then sailed North to launch an attack on Whitby. The coastguard station was hit, along with Whitby Abbey and other buildings. Again, there were civilian casualties. Other ships from the German fleet had launched an attack on Hartlepool further North causing considerable damage, many casualties and 130 deaths. There was public outrage concerning the lack of defenses and a lack of challenge by the Royal navy, whose main battleships were deployed elsewhere.

The following photos are of the Whiby Abbey ruins.

The next photo is of the part of the Abbey hit by German battlecruiser shells on the morning of 16th December 2014 during World War 1. This is where I saw a huge Angel, with wings. The emotional feelings made tears swell in my eyes, yet it wasn't until afterwards that I learnt about the attack.

CHAPTER TEN

OUR GUARDIAN ANGELS
KNOW OUR FUTURE

When I am giving someone a reading my Guardian Angel are works with their Guardian Angel. Our Guardian Angels know our Life Plan and know some of our future.

Guardian Angels won't let us see all the future. There are good reasons for this, but they will allow us an insight into some of our future.

They almost always have been many years trying to "Get Through" to the person by trying to guide them by giving them intuitive feelings every step of the way. However, in this modern materialistic world we are told that spiritual things aren't real, including the existence of Angels, so many people never listen to their intuition.

Working with the Angels on our Life Plan can help change our future for the better!

When I give someone a Life Plan reading, if the Angels are willing to help then some amazing visions unfold before my spiritual eye.

I am usually shown two versions of the future, two paths for someone. The first path is a future that would happen anyway, without my intervention. It usually has the same difficulties and challenges that a person has experienced in life up to the present, continuing as before.

The second version of the future is a path of greater happiness, life fulfilment, fewer things going wrong. I choose not to dwell on the first path, so I describe the happier, more fulfilling second path to the person I am giving a reading to.

The miracle is that as I describe the second path the Angels are working to change the person's future for the better. The second happier, more fulfilling path becomes their new future.

The moment in time that the Angels reveal an in-depth Life Plan is the pivotal moment in a person's life that changes their future for the better!

I have helped many thousands of people free of charge over the past fifteen years, using my clairvoyant gift.

My Spiritual Research is based on logical conclusions, and a belief in an amazing intelligence within the spiritual dimension that communicates through the Angels.

I am constantly guided by the Angels who work in unconditional love, and I always work using my spiritual gift of Discernment. This is the true ability to discern between good and evil. Opening oneself up to spiritual messages and visions from Heaven is risky because any enhanced spiritual awareness can also open ourselves up to the heavy negative, evil spiritual energies that are earthbound. The ability to discern comes with the knowledge that negative energies can be blocked, instructed to go away, and even dealt with by prayer. I often pray for the Angels that I call "Rescue Angels" to carry away earthbound souls to a place where they can find peace.

In addition to being given visions of the future for some people, I may also receive other messages from Heaven, through the Angels. These have been given to me over many years.

The messages are about the meaning of life and have revealed an amazing picture. This has helped me to help others which is absolutely the reason why I have been given this work.

Our future is not just simply knowing what our personal future may become but being aware that the Angels can change some of our personal future to maximise our happiness and fulfilment.

LIFE LESSONS

Our Life Plan was determined before we were born: What we would do, where we would live, people we would form a relationship with, including soulmates.

We may find ourselves making the same mistakes over, and over again. In human relationships, career, personal-finance, and all aspects of our lives. We may be told that is the fault of our Free Will, but often we seem slow to learn. Sometimes the real reason is because of our Life Lessons.

Life Lessons are worked-out and planned before we are born. These can be identified through a heightened awareness as we learn to Sense Angels. Life Lessons can also be identified by recognising the life experience of recurring unfair, difficult times such as in relationship problems.

Once our Life Lessons are identified we can change our outlook on how we tackle the future. Life lessons do not include serious illness or accident. These events are not on our life plan. The way that we can avoid these is to learn to listen to spiritual warnings that we are given through our feelings, primarily our intuition.

EXAMPLES OF LIFE LESSONS

- We might be too loving and caring so that others take advantage of us. We may therefore need to learn Tough Love for their sake as well as for ourselves

- Learning to correct our lack of Empathy and Self-Centred behaviour
- Learning to control our Anger
- Gaining experience of caring for someone
- Learning by experience of loss.
- We may also need to gain more empathy for nature and the   environment.

FREE WILL

A lot of weight is given to Free Will steering our lives. It certainly influences our everyday routine decision-making.

We may also be surrendering some of our Free Will to others, such as when we are in a personal relationship.

No matter what our Free Will does for us, or which way it leads us, our positive Life Plan events will still happen.
Future global events such as severe weather events and natural disasters can be seen through Angel visions at a personal level if that person is to travel to the affected area. Warnings can be given to avoid the situation.

SIXTH SENSE

The understanding of how and why the future can be partly seen has been a significant part of my spiritual research project over the last 40 years. Some people claim to have a "Sixth Sense". This is the ability to sense spiritually and is our Guardian Angel at work. Our Sixth Sense can give us feelings about the future.

When I give an Angel messages reading, it is often to help a grieving relative with a loved one who has passed.
However, many more people want to know what the future holds for them, and the ability to help people see some of the future is an important part of my work.
The Spiritual Realm is a place of Unconditional Love.

We may travel through life worried about the future, and sometimes feeling cold inside, because we are not feeling the love from our Guardian Angels. The society we live in does not teach how to recognise our Guardian Angels. I can show you how to re-connect with their spiritual love and guidance that will lead us to true happiness and fulfilment.

LOGICAL EXPLANATIONS

Logical discoveries through Spiritual Research are mostly not capable of being proven by science, simply because science, especially physics, is based entirely on the way our physical universe is put together. The Spiritual Realm is another dimension, with its own building blocks that cannot be measured by our physics. Both our universe, and the spiritual dimension have one major thing in common, and that is immense energy. I personally believe that, just like weighing scales, the energy of our physical universe is in balance with the energy of the spiritual dimension.

FIRST HEAVEN

As described earlier, there are many people who have had "Near Death Experiences" (NDE), and for those who wish further reading there are many books, and YouTube videos where you can see personal stories of such experiences.

The Angels have helped me see through to the beautiful place that many who have an "NDE" travel to. I call this place "First Heaven". Why? Because it is the first place most of us go when we first leave our Earthly life. It is a very real, solid place, and created in the image of the Earthly home we have just left so that we can transition into the next life. There are valleys, rivers, lakes, trees, flowers, green grass. Colours are vivid and the experience of being in that place is intense and joyful. Others who have passed may be waiting to greet us, but only where there is a bond of love or warm friendship. Dogs, cats, horses, can be seen with those who cared for them in life.

We can stay in this place for a long time, although there is no real time, but only the moment of "Now".

We will then move on to further experiences, and ultimately to be reborn into another life.

REINCARNATION

It would seem that we all have many lives. Each life is given to us for adventure, experience, challenges, and hopefully spiritual growth.

How do we achieve spiritual growth?

We grow spiritually when we become less self-centred, and more caring towards other people, towards animals, nature and the environment.

To spiritually grow is why we have many lives, and our Life Plan is reset before each life to improve on our previous lives. Our Guardian Angels know our Life Plan.

WHO ARE WE?

We are an immortal soul. Our soul energy cannot be seen because it is made of the same stuff as energies within the spiritual realm.

Over many years of giving clairvoyant readings, I see that we retain our memories, and our character when we leave our physical body and pass back home to Heaven at the end of our physical life. Our soul, the person we are, the "I", the "Me" inside each one of us is eternal.

What do those in Heaven know about our future?

Heaven is a place of infinite intelligence. We all have a Life Plan that was determined for us before we were born. Those in Heaven know our Life Plan. Those in Heaven who are closest to us in our daily lives are our Guardian Angels.

Our Life Plan would include the major events planned for our life such as whom we might meet, the work we will do, and the interests we might pursue, plus much more. When fortune tellers pick up future happenings in a person's life these are the things they might pick up. However, other things are also planned for our lives before we are born, and fortune tellers often miss these. I call them "Life Challenges". Such challenges can be hard, difficult, and make life a struggle for long periods of time. They are put in place to give us life experience, adventure, and with a purpose of helping us spiritually grow more rapidly. Spiritual Growth means to become more caring towards others, towards animals and nature, and towards the environment of our planet Earth. Those who have an inner drive, a Calling, to do what they can to reduce the effects of climate change are an example of human beings caring about our planet Earth, and the future of humanity, and nature.

Those in Heaven are living in a place of beauty, unconditional love, purpose, and oneness. This "Oneness" means that all knowledge, and everything about us, is known, and we, the person inside who we call "I" or "Me" is made of the same Conscious soul energy as the souls in Heaven.

So, what do our Guardian Angels know of our personal future?

Well, firstly they know our Life Plan and Life Challenges. Some of the Life Plan and challenges will have already happened and are now in the past. You may want a better future, and my teachings will help identify the past events that have been difficult, and then help to identify your future, and change it towards a better course, giving you potential for greater happiness and fulfilment.

Our Guardian Angels allow us to see some of the future that has already been planned, but not everything. To pick up what they are prepared to show us concerning our personal future we need to learn how to live our lives feeling and resonating more closely with them. I have devoted an entire chapter of this book to help you learn to identify and work with your Guardian Angel. This is extremely important in my teachings, and if you follow it through this alone may change your life in a positive way forever!

The infinite intelligence of Heaven includes a knowingness of what everyone is doing. Imagine some huge computer program that combines events and stores the information of over seven billion people so that it can give the intelligent loving Source in Heaven, whom religions may call "God", a picture of the future.
The Source can also see events happing in nature, and to planet Earth. We may be given some of this picture, but only as they think we need, via our Guardian Angels. This view of the future will come as "Premonitions". The world will become a better and safer place if human beings could universally accept the existence of our Guardian Angels, and then learn how to listen to them.

What spoils the plan, and what makes the world so blind? The answer is negative energy. The human beings who are totally self-centred, and totally lacking in empathy for other people, and for animals, nature, and the environment, are totally disconnected from their personal Guardian Angel. Guardian Angels resonate closely with us when we are caring and loving and will not help us if we are self-centred.

Those in Heaven can see what people who are filled with negative, self-centred energy. Heaven can see what they are doing, and what they are likely to do. Those in Heaven cannot get through to such people because the main channel of communication is through our Guardian Angels.

Those in Heaven therefore get through to people who are resonating more closely with their Guardian Angels, to give them feelings, awareness, and a "Calling" to do what they can to work against the destruction caused by the self-centred ones.
If self-centred behaviour is at the heart of those in government of a nation, then everyone suffers. Alternatively, if those in government have policies of care towards others then many of the citizens of a nation will have more personal freedom, and a better quality of life.

CHAPTER ELEVEN

Discovering the Meaning of Life

Most human beings have their own spiritual beliefs. However, if you wish to learn how to sense Angels it means learning the "System" of how the Spiritual Realm works, as I teach. My ability to sense Angels came to me inadvertently following many years of research into the meaning of life. These same discoveries have withstood the test of time for me and have proven essential to my ongoing understanding of the spiritual visions and messages that I receive.

I urge you to understand this "System", and I feel that as you assimilate this knowledge you may begin to understand the true "Bigger Picture" and start to "Open-up" clairvoyantly.

For me personally, understanding the System is an absolute in my interpreting the visions that I experience. The Spiritual System has been the subject of my research for more than 40 years. Sometimes the visions the Angels give me are powerful, sometimes faint. The energies that I perceive can overwhelm the senses or be faint energies at the extreme periphery of perception. By understanding the System, I know what the Angels are trying to communicate. The meaning and significance of visions can be interpreted and made sense of correctly.

The System Outline

There are two main universes: the physical universe, and the spiritual universe of the Heavens. Their energies balance each other.

The spiritual universe has its own laws of physics that cannot be detected by the science of our physical universe.

The spiritual universe is an almost infinite, vast energy, and is a conscious intelligence. I call it the dimension of "Conscious Energy".

Our soul, the person we call "I" or "Me", is made of conscious energy. Our true home is in Heaven.

There is a vast intelligence at the centre of the spiritual universe, a source of all creation and purpose. We are born out of this "Source" (whom religions may name "God").

When we are in the spiritual universe the energy that we feel, almost like air that we breathe, is that of unconditional love.

We will live through many lives over thousands of years. The purpose of each life is for adventure, experience, and to spiritually grow more caring and loving of other souls, and Creation. We eventually end up merging back into the Source.

There are many Angels in the spiritual universe of the Heavens. Angels have many different roles. Their purpose is to help care for us, and for nature, and for the planet.

We each have at least one Angel dedicated to helping us. We can describe such Angels as "Guardian Angels" or "Angel Guides".

After each life we have a period of spiritual rest, and a life review. We may stop for many years (although there is no time in the spiritual universe) and look over those still in life whom we love. At some point it will be necessary to move on within the spiritual realm, probably in readiness for being born again into a new life.

Before each life, we are given a "Life Plan". A Life Plan will include things we will do in life, people we will meet, plus much more. We are also set "Life Challenges". Such challenges will be difficult, but we will learn much from the experiences, and hopefully become a better person.

After we are born, our memory of Heaven is forgotten, and our Life Plan, and Life Challenges are not held in our conscious mind. However, our Guardian Angels know these plans and challenges, and will try to help us throughout life. The secret is learning to be closer to our Guardian Angels so that we can sense the help they try to give us.

Our Angels try to help people in the following ways:
They are a link between ourselves and our loved ones in Heaven
They are a channel for healing
They know our life situation, and will try to help and guide us
They know some of our future, and will allow us to see some of our future
They may bring us premonitions concerning the future.

My early spiritual experiences

Have you ever had a spiritual experience and perhaps a sense of your Guardian Angel? This can sometimes happen when we are seriously ill and near death. I describe my own experience of being with my Guardian Angel in Heaven whilst I was fighting for life in hospital.

A ten-month old baby struggling for life with severe life-threatening asthma could be observed lying in a cot in an oxygen tent. The location was a hospital in the city of Bradford, Yorkshire, England. The year was 1951.

The baby was me, and up to the age of 10 months I had been a healthy baby but having been given a childhood vaccine the day before, I now had suffered an immune system reaction, and started with severe asthma that could not be brought under control.

The police officer knocked loudly on the front door of a Victorian terrace house in the city of Bradford, Yorkshire, England, and the city was enveloped by a heavy fog of mist and smoke from the industry powered by coal, coal fires warming the houses, and the local chimneys of cotton mills and woollen mills. The locals gave a name for this pollution as "Smog".

It was late evening, and a young couple apprehensively opened the door to a male police officer who said, "We have just received a call from the hospital. Your baby son is near death and won't survive the night". Very few people had a home telephone in 1951. Telephones were a luxury of the wealthy, very few people owned a car, and in the years soon after World War Two most people didn't have many of the things that we take for granted in the 21st century.

The young couple were my parents, and I was the baby. I had been a fit and healthy baby, but a diphtheria vaccination triggered severe asthma which hospitalised me, leaving me struggling for life lying in a cot in an oxygen tent.

My parents were only allowed to visit once weekly, and then only to observe me through a glass window to help prevent infection. This appeared to be the procedure throughout my time in hospital – over eighteen months. The police called at my parents' home on several occasions throughout that period because I was near to death.

My parents caught the first bus available next morning to the hospital, feeling distraught, only to find with joy and much emotion that I had made a significant recovery and was no longer in danger.

This was the first time that I had been close to death, but I continued to have recurrent severe asthma attacks with all the crisis that an asthma attack brings.

Do infants remember their lives at such a young age? My detailed memory of all this is not there, but I do clearly remember times when I was no longer in my body but in a warm secure loving place with a loving spiritual being. My speech as an infant wasn't fully developed but the feelings were that I was rescued from my suffering body and had spent a lot of time with this beautiful being. I was then sent back to my body and immediately experienced the suffering again. I remember feeling "I don't want to go back", only to be told "You have to go back".

Looking back on this time now, I realise that the beautiful loving being is my Guardian Angel. We all have a Guardian Angel, and in this book, I will explain how these beautiful beings stay with us and try to help us throughout our lives and beyond this life.

What were my memories of this time? I remember being with a loving Angel figure, no wings, just a beautiful loving being who cared for me. Most of the time I felt no suffering, but existed in a secure place, surrounded by love. I knew I was somewhere else, not in the body of that suffering infant. I didn't want to go back into my body, but somehow, I had to. There was no language in communicating this to me, just feelings, just a "Knowingness".

I was left with permanent asthma. I would get frequent attacks, and symptoms became acute with exercise, so I could never participate in sport. I missed half of my school life and was always a sickly child. However, like many people with a disability, I eventually became more determined to succeed than most, and achieved high grades in school, before leaving in my mid-teens to pursue a career in accountancy.

Throughout my childhood the experience of being with my Guardian Angel, and still feeling my Guardian Angel with me was constant. I failed to understand violence. Why do some children start fights and cause hurt? Why does it give some children pleasure to bully others? Why do children cause psychological hurt to others by calling them names? Why do children and adults cause pain to others – isn't there enough pain in daily survival?

Of course, I understand now that much of this behaviour is a part of growing up, but such behaviour for many, many people is still there in adulthood. We live in a world that is advanced in science but suffers much spiritually primitive behaviour caused by many adults. Often those in positions of power and authority have attained their positions by walking over others. Alternatively, authority and leadership can, of course, be attributed to "Survival of the fittest". This would imply that spiritual forces at work might intend that to happen.

However, throughout my childhood, into adult life, and still to this day I realise two things:

1) Sometimes we cannot help hurting others – life throws situations at us daily. How we react and respond can never be perfect.

2) Should we deliberately hurt others, if we are too self-centred and have little empathy for others, then this causes hurt and is spiritually wrong.

My awareness of Guardian Angels opened a door to my spiritual senses and my enhanced intuitive feelings became a normal part of my life.

However, living in a modern world of science, materialism, and new technological advances, I found conflict with my spiritual experiences. My logical mind had to find proof of my spirituality. I am an accountant, I have a car, computers, and immerse myself fully in the world around.

Of course, I was born into a world where science rules. Historically science and religion have been at total odds with each other. I use the word "Religion" because almost all spiritual beliefs are classified as either "Religious beliefs and experiences" being good, and every other spiritual experience as being bad.

THE ARCHANGEL

On a beautiful Spring morning, 1st May 1999 I awoke at 6am to find sunshine penetrating the curtains.

As I lay resting in bed, realising this was a Saturday morning and thinking that I don't have to get up for work, something wonderful happened. A spiritual face appeared in front of me. The face was that of an Archangel. I felt fearful, but then a reassuring feeling came across from this incredible Being who was radiating golden light. His face was itself a golden light. The eyes were what drew my attention. A feeling that He knew everything about me, but understood, and that He forgave my mistakes and imperfections. His love was, and is, unconditional. This book isn't about religion. I am a Christian, having been baptised in the Church of England as a baby and then baptised again with a fundamental Church in Keighley, Yorkshire at the age of nineteen years. For most of my life I hadn't attended Church, but still tried to live a Christian lifestyle. Although I knew I had some "Sixth Sense", I had always been very sceptical of clairvoyants, mediums, psychics, and fortune tellers. Firstly, Christians don't approve of what they do. Secondly my logical mind simply thought of them as nonsense. This same logical mind had spent a lifetime trying to find the meaning of life. Although by profession I am an accountant, I had made an amateur study of astronomy, astrophysics, and quantum physics. I subscribed to the magazine "New Scientist", avidly devouring the latest scientific discoveries and theories. I had studied religious beliefs. I loved nature. Dogs, cats, horses, rabbits, birds, all animals to me seemed to have someone inside looking out. It isn't just human beings who have a soul. The trees, flowers, plants, and all of nature, seem to vibrate with a life-giving energy from a divine source. Equally importantly I had also listened to people. I listened to real life experiences. So many ordinary people over the years would recount their own real-life experiences of ghosts. On every occasion I was always very willing to listen because to me there was a need to evaluate the situation. Old ladies would tell me how they knew their deceased husband was still close by. All of these things are spiritual experiences that Christians must deny. All these things are largely ignored by many people in modern, scientific, materialistic societies. They think about education, career, work, family, things to buy, holidays, sport. All these are good, normal things. All are a part of life. Then when someone they know and love passes from life they are thrown into a desolate place of grief and loss, with no answers from anyone.

What is it all about?

So now, here I am, lying in bed with the face of a Heavenly Being, an Archangel, in front of me. I heard no words but just knew instantly what I was being told. I suddenly felt myself rising-up at great speed to enter a new dimension and saw before me a beautiful place. "This is First Heaven" was the knowledge implanted in my thoughts. What I saw before me I will now describe.

Firstly, I will describe the feelings. At first, I sensed a pleasant caressing feeling of gentle warmth. This grew quickly into a feeling of love. Yes, I could FEEL love as something tangible. I realised that love was all around just like the air we breathe. I felt at ease in this relaxed atmosphere of love. I began to understand this was what some people describe as "Unconditional Love". I felt important and loved even though I knew I was far from perfect.

This new dimension is very real. I could see a rock-solid landscape of a green valley before my eyes. It struck me how vivid the colours hit my vision everywhere I turned, with vivid shades of green grass, the leaves of trees, and every shade of flower vibrating in the beauty and aura of an eternal Spring morning. The colours of the flowers were of yellow, red, purple, white, and each flower seemed to glow with an aura of life energy. A gentle breeze seemed to move the grass, the trees, and the flowers. I could see real people, not grey, transparent ghosts, but real people wearing normal clothing! Their clothing was in normal colours. Real animals were moving around just ignoring me because they had no fear, because there is no fear in Heaven. Some were wild animals. Others were pets, mainly dogs, cats, and one or two horses, and obviously were there to accompany some of the people I could see. The most noticeable feeling within the feeling of love was of the profound beauty of this new "World", this other dimension that is more real than the physical earth we live on. I felt a familiarity as if I had arrived back home after an adventure into the earth plane. I didn't think to look at myself, my hands or feet, but felt my personality as my normal self, but with a profound sense of well-being, and a floating feeling with no discomfort, no pain. People were walking around yet I felt they could simply move to some other place if they wanted, through their thoughts.

I could see houses like on Earth, as if they were there to give a feeling of being at home to those who had passed. I could also see in the distance beautiful white buildings. I was stood in this lush green valley, and the nearest building was a thatched farmhouse. A man and his wife emerged from the farmhouse to look at me. I got the feeling that this was the same type of house they had lived in whilst in the physical world. Elsewhere in the valley people were busy, but at a steady pace. Some were gardening, tending to the flowers. I asked the Heavenly Being who was still with me where was everyone else? There should surely be many millions of people in Heaven. I could only see perhaps thirty or forty people. The answer came instantly with a clear vision in my thoughts of many people simply resting in the white buildings in the distance. Also, that there are many valleys, and many, many different places in this very real dimension. I didn't know at the time that I would come to see many of these other places in my future role as a clairvoyant.

I noticed the sky was a hazy blue, yet an all-pervading brightness and energy emanated from above. I wondered if above the place I was visiting there was a higher place. My thoughts were instantly read! "Come, I will show you this Higher place," said this Heavenly Being. I then found myself flying upwards at speed into the sky through a barrier of white, almost like cloud, to emerge into another level of Heaven, which I now call "Second Heaven". This dimension is incredibly bright. This dimension wasn't a solid real world like the lower dimension of Heaven. It was as if I was floating in a brilliant white mist with no sign of ground or sky or distance. White radiant Beings were busy working. They could be described as Angels without wings. I knew what they were doing. They were organising everything, keeping both the dimension of Heaven, and the physical dimension supported. Above them I saw a sky of brilliant white light and felt an overwhelming and infinite energy of warmth and unconditional love. This energy was a vast loving intelligence, yet with the oneness of a person. A person who is neither a "He" nor a "She". This was the infinitely divine person who is the source of all knowledge, intelligence, meaning and purpose. I realised that this Divine Consciousness of He/ She is the Oneness, connected to the "Me" or "I" inside each one of us. This Light above me was the Source, the Creator, the centre of purity and of love and purpose. This Light above me was God. I call the Highest Heaven "Third Heaven".

I looked and received smiles of love from some of the Angelic Beings nearby. They were very busy working, looking after life, and very intent in their purpose.

The Heavenly Being who accompanied me was Spiritually Higher than the Angels for I knew that they were looking at Him with respect as a part of the Highest spiritual authority, a part of God. There was a feeling of the Heavenly Being having much, much more work to do, and that it was time for me to go. I didn't realise that from now on in my work on Earth I would catch glimpses of this place many times again. The Heavenly Being concluded the visit with a message:

"I will now leave you and I grant you the full spiritual gift of CLAIRVOYANCE to see the spiritual realm. I also pass to you the gift of spiritual discernment, to have the wisdom to discern between good and evil spirits.

Your work will be to help others with these spiritual gifts, for the world is in much need of spiritual understanding and direction".

I immediately found myself back in bed again. The time had moved from 6am to 6.30am. That half hour changed my life forever.

What happens when we pass across to the Heaven? The following account is fictional but incorporates most of the experiences that we can go through.

Peter

Peter struggled for breath as he walked along the path towards his home. He had just finished work and thought he had a bad case of indigestion because of pains in his chest. Sweat was pouring down his face, and he was beginning to feel exhausted. He was angry. His girlfriend, and partner of seven years, had just finished their relationship and she had moved out of their rented home to live with someone she met at her work.

Stressful thoughts and feelings were going around his head making him angry and depressed.

His father had died of a sudden heart attack when he was only twelve years old, leaving his mother to finish bringing him up.

Cruel cancer had recently taken the life of his mother just six months earlier. This made it even harder to bear the loss of his girlfriend as well.
Suddenly his chest was gripped, as if in a vice. He fell to the floor. Then all went black.
He was on a public road and someone had seen him and called for help. It wasn't too long before paramedics arrived.
Peter wouldn't have known that the rare heart condition that had taken the life of his father at a young age was genetic and had now claiming a second victim.

Peter suddenly found himself awake. He was looking down on a scene of commotion below. An ambulance, and people milling around someone laid out on the ground. He had died. He felt free, not just free of the heaviness of a body struggling to keep going every day, not just free of the pain across his chest, but free of the anger, free of the emotions that had taken over his life in recent months.

A beautiful light appeared, and he felt himself being pulled towards the light by some invisible force. Yet, he didn't feel afraid. He knew that his spirit was free and somehow all the cares and worries of his everyday life disappeared. He realised that he had died but for some reason wasn't bothered. He didn't want to go back into life. As Peter fell into the light a vortex in the shape of a tunnel emerged and he was drawn at high speed towards the tunnel. He found himself moving through this swirling vortex at high speed with a sense of anticipation, and a profound feeling of love surrounding him. He felt the love surrounding and protecting him as he began to perceive another light which gradually became brighter and brighter. It was the most beautiful light he had ever seen, and he felt totally at ease. There now appeared an Angel at the end of the tunnel. The vision became clearer, and he realised that his Guardian Angel was waiting to meet him.
Peter emerged suddenly from the vortex of the tunnel into

a beautiful garden. He immediately recognised two people. "Mum...Dad, you're here to meet me!"

"We love you, so much, son," said his father. Mum smiled and gave him a hug. An embrace, that became two souls merging, through the binding love of mother and son.

"You pushed yourself too hard," his mum commented. "We were watching over you. You should have got yourself checked out for any heart problems knowing how your father passed".

Peter was still trying to familiarise himself with his new surroundings. It somehow didn't matter to him that his life was over. He remembered an old saying "Life is but a moment". This place he was in now was so beautiful. He felt alive, and the air he breathed was an atmosphere of love beyond description.

Mum explained that she and dad had a home here – just like the family home back in the physical world. Then his thoughts made him laugh as he said to his dad: "This place is more real than the world we lived in!". Beyond the garden he could now see the family home, and in the distance were beautiful mountains. He could see the landscape of a green valley, and nearby flowers danced in a delicate breeze as their colours radiated in vivid splendour far more intense than on Earth. What surprised him was that everything was real, solid, with vibrant colours. Heaven isn't a misty, intangible place. Animals are across there in Heaven, but they have no fear and simply ignored the human souls and continued grazing in the lush grass. People who cared for pets such as dogs, cats, and horses appeared to have these much-loved animals with them. The love bond between a person and that of their devoted pet shone out as a connection that spans the dimensions of Earth and Heaven.

Peter realised that Heaven was a familiar place. He had been here before. It was like coming home.

"What happens next, mum?" was Peter's question after what seemed like an eternity in simply taking-in the beauty of his surroundings.

His mum replied "Well, in your case we've been told there won't be much rest. Many souls like your dad and I can spend as long as we wish just resting. However, the Guardian Angels have told us that they have an urgent mission for you. This mission will be shared by many souls who are like you".

Sleep fell upon Peter. He awoke to see a beautiful woman stood next to him. "Julia, Julia, is that you?"
A woman who appeared to be in her early thirties, dark flowing hair, and a flowing silver dress that shimmered like stars. Her smile was captivating. Her eyes showed a depth of love and compassion that reflected an eternal bond.
"Peter, I have been waiting for you for many years"
With sudden recognition Peter said: "You are, or should I say you were my wife!". "Oh, my beautiful Julia. I never thought I would see you again!"
Peter then began to feel disorientated. "I didn't have a wife, I was single. My girlfriend had just split up with me".
"Come with me," said Julia. "Those who have recently left the physical realm often feel confused. You need a time of peace and adjustment. Come, take my hand".

Peter joined hands with Julia and felt himself lifted up as if he weighed nothing, and was flying over beautiful valleys, houses, and a landscape so beautiful beyond any imagination. Eventually they came to rest along the shore of a lake. Contrasting shades of light shimmered in the lake before them. The movement created patterns that appeared to be alive in dancing with the joy and beauty of this place. Feelings of peace and love were overwhelming.

"I was your wife in your previous life," said Julia. "We were married for over forty years. You died in 1970. I lived on until 1983. After I passed across to Heaven, I didn't want another life. You are my soulmate and I just wanted to wait here for you. You always were a determined soul and volunteered for another life to be born in 1989, even though you were warned that it would only be a short life because of the genetic heart defect from your

Earth parents."

"How come you know me as Peter?"

Julia laughed. "You were named Peter as my husband. When you were born into a new life in 1989, I whispered in the ear of your Earth parents to name you Peter, and fortunately they seemed to feel that was the name to give you. You will learn that those in spirit, such as ourselves, can whisper in the ear of those in the physical realm, but they don't always listen!" Julia laughed. "You never listened. I couldn't get through to you no matter how hard I tried!"

An eternity of peace, love, companionship of soulmates now seemed to pass as the two sat beside this lake of beauty and tranquillity. Time does not exist in the reality of Heaven. The only time is that of "The Now", "The Moment", "The Instant". Without the clutter of thoughts and worries about yesterday or tomorrow the time of "Now" becomes incredibly intense. Peter thought to himself. How he wished he had realised the value of appreciating every moment, every second of his physical life on Earth. What a lesson that would have been in reducing his stress and worries, and of intensifying his everyday experience. Julia suddenly spoke: "I agree". Peter laughed realising that they were as one and their thoughts and feelings were shared.

Peter fell asleep. We can sleep in Heaven for our souls still need to rest. Julia woke him to ask if he felt ready to move on.

"Our Guardian Angels have told me that we will soon have a meeting to attend," said Julia. "First, you must go to the Library for your life review."

Peter remembered the Library from his previous lives. A brilliant white building filled with books. Peter had lived in the digital age when books were becoming less in printed version, and everything available online. Yet the Library still looked like shelves filled with printed books.

An Angel, not his Guardian Angel, appeared and stood alongside Peter. "I am your Angel Guide," said the radiant soul who had the appearance of a kind but strict elderly teacher. "My name is Matthew, and it is time to review the life you have just been through."

Peter could see a book with his name on it.

Matthew said, "You lived a good life as a very caring person. You did make one or two mistakes. Turn to page 23, and you'll see a date of May 31st, 2010".

Peter opened the page. As he opened the page it became alive like a video, and then suddenly he was pulled into the scene. It was May 31st, 2010, and he had received a phone call to inform him that his closest friend Gary was in hospital. Peter had been too busy with his own problems to visit him and had not fully realised how Gary had missed his friend in his time of need.

Matthew said: "You can't put things right, Peter. You can see and feel how hurt Gary was because you ignored his needs."

Peter realised that he was being taught a lesson. Life on Earth is like a school. We are all there for the experiences that life throws at us, and to learn to be as caring and loving of others around us as possible, even in the hardest of times.

"Don't worry," said Matthew. "You are quite an advanced soul. There were not many times in your life when you didn't show care and love for others. You can imagine how many souls find this a very harrowing time as they review lives that in some cases showed disregard and lack of love and care for people around. Where they caused deliberate hurt then they are made aware of the pain they caused, be it emotional or physical pain. Your life review has been easy, and over much more quickly than that of many others!"

As Peter left the Library with Matthew, Julia joined them. The Light of the Source that religions may call "God" shone above. A Light that is brighter than any light in the physical universe yet does not dazzle. The energy from the Light is of pure unconditional love. Peter couldn't help but feel that he was a part of, and connected to everything, and that the entire spiritual universe was joined together as just one infinitely vast oneness. Peter suddenly knew that all human beings, and all animals have a soul energy connected to the "Oneness". He realised that the spiritual life energies that look after trees, plants, flowers, insects, and the Earth, are all connected with the "Oneness". Peter knew instantly that to hurt any part of the "Oneness" was like hurting oneself.

A place of Angels

"Come with me" said The Angel Matthew. Peter and Julia found themselves travelling at great speed away from First Heaven to somewhere in Heaven they hadn't been before. They found themselves in a Place of Angels. Matthew reminded them that before their previous life as human beings they had rested in First Heaven, so it was necessary to give them both some knowledge of the other Heavens.

A vision unfolded before them of how those in the spiritual dimension of Heaven had created the physical universe 13.8 billion Earth years ago. Heaven had created millions of stars that were clustered into numerous galaxies. Planets were created to orbit many of the stars and Heaven created some planets to support life. Peter and Julia realised that discoveries by scientists on Earth were just the discovery of the science that already existed. The infinite creative intelligence of Heaven was revealed to them.

Angels are messengers from Heaven. They are the link between human beings and Heaven. The Place of Angels where Peter and Julia now stood was the gathering place of Angels whose work it is to support human beings and all of life on Earth. "There are other places where advanced spiritual beings who are not Angels work in creating life," said Matthew. "Your mission is to work with the Angels in saving planet Earth, humanity and nature from the worst consequences of Climate Change."

Peter and Julia glided effortlessly in amongst the Angels who were of many types and appearances.

Some had a human appearance and radiated a beautiful soul energy. These were the Guardian Angels that accompany all human beings in life. They have special abilities and energies to exist in both Heaven and Earth at the same time. Other Angelic Beings were seen shimmering in soul energy of different colours. Their shape kept changing and Matthew told Peter and Julia they could appear to human beings with a radiance resembling wings.

"Angels have many different jobs," said Matthew. Peter and Julia were told that Healing Angels are specialised in giving new, healing, Life Energies to human beings, animals, and all of life in nature. "People often feel that they aren't helped by the Healing Angels, but without their Life Energies healing would not occur, and life would cease to exist," said Matthew.

Angels Guiding People

"Can I speak with some of the Angels?" asked Julia. The affirmative response from Matthew found Julia and Peter suddenly near a Guardian Angel with a female appearance who already knew the question that Julia was asking. "My name is Anna" said the Guardian Angel. Then, like a video Julia and Peter saw how Anna was guiding a young lady age in her late teens. "I can get through to her easily" said Anna. "I work through her feelings and intuition so well because she is a good, caring soul. I have guided her and put things in place in her life to help her become a nurse. Her caring nature is much appreciated by her patients. I have guided her to find a like-minded soul as a partner in life. They both care passionately for animals and nature and spend their spare time volunteering for an animal rescue charity. They also care passionately about beautiful planet Earth and are campaigning for a rapid change by society to move away from reliance on fossil fuels and prevent the further harmful consequences to all of life caused by climate change."

Julia and Peter then found themselves near another Guardian Angel with a male appearance. "I am Mark" said the Guardian Angel. "I look over several souls, but one of them, a man aged in his late forties, won't listen. We are all given Free Will to make our own choices. He has always ignored his conscience and the intuitive feelings that I try to send him. His soul is so much cut off from Heaven that he allows negative energies to influence his soul. He blames everyone but himself for the way that his life has gone wrong. He was a psychological bully to his wife, and so she left him. He has never shown any love or care towards his children who are now adults. He only ever cares about himself. He once had a pet dog that he mistreat and one of his children took it off him. He doesn't care about nature. At work he was successful in his career because he was quite ruthless and blocked the career paths of others around him." "How will his life be judged?" asked Julia. Mark replied: "When he eventually passes back to First Heaven his life review will present him with the mistakes and hurt that he caused. His next incarnation as a human being will be planned to give him the challenges and the opportunities to become more caring".

Finally, Julia and Peter found themselves near another Guardian Angel of female appearance. " I am Sunlight" she told them. Her energy seemed much brighter than the other Guardian Angels. "That's why they call me Sunlight" she said, as if knowing what Julia was about to ask.

"I get some of the difficult cases that don't progress." said Sunlight. " My energies are better developed because I am an older soul who has been working as a Guardian Angel for much longer than some of the others". "I will show you how I help people" said Sunlight. Again, almost like a video, Julia and Peter were shown a man in his early thirties called Ben. He had been member of criminal gang whilst in his early teenage years, and was involved with fights and crime. "No Guardian Angel could get through to him" said Sunlight. "So I got involved. What I did was to work through the intuitive feelings of an older man who ran a local store. I steered the older man with feelings that he could help Ben. This older man offered Ben a job working in the store. Ben had been unable to find work. He had not passed exams at school and came from a household of a family torn by divorced parents and poverty. Ben became impressed by the kindness of the owner of the local store. He learnt that if he worked he could earn money and pull away from his life with the gang. "I suddenly found one day that Ben listened to me" said Sunlight. "I managed to get through to him by projecting feelings that he could sense intuitively. I have guided him, with the help of the kindly store owner. I placed opportunities on Ben's path that he grasped. He went to college and gained engineering qualifications and is now in a job earning good money as an engineer. Ben has married a good woman, and learnt how to treat her with love, care and respect."

"Does this mean that Ben's soul has seen spiritual development and grown?" asked Julia. "That's right", said Sunlight. "If people can learn to spiritually grow, do less harm to others and nature, and learn to show care and love, then these are some of the main purposes of life as a human being."

A Calling

"What is our mission?" asked Peter. The Angel Matthew replied: "We need you both, and many others, to volunteer for another life as a human being on Earth. In this new life you will be allowed to retain some of your memories of Heaven. We are giving you both, and the others a special "Calling" to dedicate yourselves to influencing society around you to change direction, to change the way of life for people, so that the environment and nature will no longer be damaged by human actions. It will take many souls like yourselves to complete this most urgent purpose. We will start to guide you when you reach an age where you can make change happen. We will guide you through your intuitive feelings, and by putting things in place in your life to make positive change happen". "Will we be together?" asked Julia. Matthew replied: "You won't be together in childhood. However, you will both have strong feelings that you need to seek out your eternal soulmate. We will put things in place so that you meet each other in your late teenage years. The rest is to be decided by your individual free will, but I feel confident that you will spend the rest of that life together and you both will be guided to work to help save nature and the environment. Remember, we will be guiding you, and you will both be aware of that."

.

CHAPTER TWELVE

First Heaven

Understanding who and what we are, and why we are given life is an absolute foundation in understanding our lives so far and sorting out what the future holds for us.
Understanding the System that manages life and the afterlife gives a true insight into why all events, past, present and future happen.

In unity with many religions, the clairvoyant experience is one of seeing "Heaven" as a place from which unconditional love emanates. There is definitely a "Oneness" of all soul energy culminating in the ultimate Source that I still call "God" from my Christian upbringing, and the many years spent in my adult life as an active Christian. However, the real images I see as a clairvoyant "Seeing through to Heaven" differ from most descriptions of Heaven by religious teachings.

What Does Heaven Look Like?

I name the first place we go to when we pass away from physical life "First Heaven".

It can be seen clairvoyantly as a very real, solid dimension, more real, and with a more intense experience than our physical world.

There are gardens, beautiful valleys, trees, grass, flowers. Vivid Colours. Animals may appear as animals with no fear, and no aggression. People can still appear as people, although we mainly appear in our soul state as what we are – intelligent conscious energy.

Heaven allows our soul to rest after the end of physical life. One of my first discoveries, which came as a huge surprise to me, is that the first place many of us will reach is a place that may be like our home in life, and similar to the world around that we knew in life. This is to help us transition and not feel unease at what has happened in the process of so called "Death" where we find ourselves still able to see and hear. We still have feelings, and we can still think. We realise that we are still the same person with our memories intact, although worries and stress are no longer there. I will explain the reason for this later.

The following is a true account concerning the parents of a lady I was giving an Angel messages reading:

Anne came to see me. I was given a message via my Guardian Angel that her adult daughter was having a difficult time with life. This proved to be the case because her daughter's husband had recently died, suspected suicide. What came through on the reading was a message from this husband saying it was an unintentional combination of his medical condition, diabetes, and alcohol abuse that had caused his death. The following week Anne came back to see me with her daughter. The messages from the deceased husband helped ease the pain, and then a message came through from Anne's mother. I firstly gave Anne a description of her mother. My Guardian Angel helps me with a vision of the deceased person, often in great detail. As usual I gave a full description including that of hairstyle, hair colour, height and build and clothing. I was then given a vision of Anne's mother and father living in a cottage in Wales with beautiful mountain scenery nearby. This seemed strange because Anne had an obvious Yorkshire accent, and we were in East Yorkshire. Anne, however, was amazed at the description of the home in Wales. She told me that she was Welsh, and her parents had lived in the family home in Wales, as described by me, until the death of her father. Anne's mother had spent the final years of her life living with Anne In Yorkshire.

Amidst all the emotions of Anne and her daughter there was a healing process. It was only afterwards that I thought about her mother and father still together in a home that resembled their family home in Wales. The house was real, yet I knew that they were in Heaven. They were not ghosts haunting the real physical home in Wales. Heaven had given them the familiar home surroundings to be together for as long as they needed as they transition from their needs as human beings carried with them from their Earthly lives. I often find that loving parents remain in this transition place for another reason, and that is so that can still look over the lives of children or other loved ones still in physical life. We don't stay in these surroundings forever, but certainly if we wish, perhaps until our loved ones on Earth have eventually passed-on from their lives as human beings.

My logical, spiritual research indicates that there are quantum energies that connect the dimension of the physical universe and the spiritual dimension of Heaven. These energies cross back and forth between dimensions and can replicate physical landscapes and houses on Earth. I have seen this many times whilst receiving visions. I am suspicious that some of the energies theorised in quantum physics such as dark energy and dark matter might be inter-dimensional energies of enormous proportions. Physicists have been unable to identify these energies but know they exist. Perhaps it takes something beyond physical science to identify non-physical energies inter-acting with the physical universe.

A lady called Margaret came to see me for an Angel messages

reading. As usual, I asked her to tell me nothing, other than confirm or deny the visions and messages that the Angels gave me.

"I see your mother who must be in spirit". Margaret replied "Yes"". I then went in to give a description of her appearance and how she had died. Margaret then asked me "Where is my mother now?". I can't ask questions, but the vision suddenly changed to an image of her deceased mother sat in a comfortable chair in her lounge, knitting and watching television. "That's exactly how my mother would spend the happy, restful times", said Margaret. I then went on to describe the lounge in more detail. I could see an unusual light fitting, a chandelier. Margaret was astonished. I described the chandelier in more detail. "No-one could know that and especially because the chandelier was a one-off design" she said.

Again, this reading and the visions held a different slant for me as a spiritual researcher. Heaven is real and when I say that I mean a very real, solid-looking dimension. I can conclude that the mirror image of energies from the physical world can be made to produce the same familiar surroundings and objects that were around us whilst in physical life. Also, that the spiritual universe is one of unimaginable intelligence and creative ability. I then went on to relay a vision that the Angels gave me from Margaret's father. I gave a brief description of him, and how he had died of a heart attack, which Margaret confirmed as correct. I then received a further vision of him happily working under the bonnet of a red car which he seemed quite proud of. It had the appearance of a high-powered performance vehicle. The message accompanying the vision was that I was seeing what was doing in real time. Margaret was again astonished at such a clear vision and the mention of the car. "He spent all of his spare time working on cars as a hobby. The red car was his favourite!"

Following my life changing experience with Archangel, I call the first place that our soul reaches after our physical life ends: "First Heaven".

First Heaven

I see light everywhere
Gentle warmth of unconditional love
I am drawn into First Heaven, somehow
Just here, not above

I am free from life on Earth
From pain, suffering, happiness, pleasure
Back to my true home, somehow familiar
I cannot measure
.... The overwhelming love

Yes! I can still think and see, still same old me,
I see my loved ones who passed before,
waiting here for me
I see their faces, young again,
Together we fly free
Across beautiful valleys, green grass, trees, flowers
A very real Heaven created by the One with powers
Of Creation

In the afterlife of Heaven, we will at some point have a Life Review, accompanied by our Guardian Angel. Those who have hurt others are shown and made to feel the hurt they caused. This is a true form of Justice for those who thought they had

"Got Away" with bad deeds by not being punished whilst alive as a human being. We are also shown the good things that we did. Loving and helping others, nature and the environment helps our growth and advancement as a spiritual being. Some people experience a "Life Review" before a meeting of "Wise Beings". Others may experience their Life Review in what can only be described as a "Library" in Heaven.

A Library in Heaven

My soul set free from my body, my life
I float on a path towards a building white,
The Heaven I hoped for shines all around
I breathe air of love, see beauty profound.

Heaven is light, love, joy and peace
Beauty, safety, I feel wonderful, at ease
I see radiant Angels, sense power
of the Creator above
Overwhelming, infinite, unconditional love.

Heaven offers rest, to recover from life's pain
Then time to review, start learning again.

A brilliant white building in front of me
Is a place of further learning, a Library?
I see before me many books of life
For everyone who ever lived
their toils, their strife,
Their joy, sorrow, happiness, fun,
The times they had to fight, battles lost and won.

I see a book now, with my name bold and clear
Should I reach to grasp it?
My Angel guide says "Don't fear"

Each page is a day of your life we did give
Every moment, every minute
I may view and relive.

I open a page of happiness and joy
Go back to my childhood when I was a boy,
My Angel guide told me, in a most gentle way
to visit a page where my life went astray.
Did I hurt others?
I was blind but now see
I now feel the hurt, caused directly by me.

I can enter the page, and I'm in life again
At that moment in time when I caused someone pain
I can work it through differently
Not self-centred, but care,
Understand how others feel,
Learn how to share.

I awoke, it was dawn,
Was this a vision, had I dreamed?
I'm alive, not passed away
To the afterlife that seemed so real.

Visions of the Future

Visions of the Future can be massive and overwhelm the senses of vision, communication and experience. Such visions can also be faint and fleeting, but with an understanding of the System the visions are not lost.

When I see the future, my Guardian Angel gives visions of some things that will happen, and visions of some things that may or may not happen. If I see something bad, I ask Heaven to "Block" it from happening, or make it somehow easier to deal with. I try to encourage good positive futures by using my own energies in that purpose.

Tunnel Vision

Deep-seated personal feelings within many of us about what we want to achieve, who we want to be, and the type of persons we want to be close to in our future.

These feelings were acquired by our soul before we were born. Those with Tunnel Vision succeed when others who don't keep hold of that focus don't succeed.

The following is a story of three brothers. As in most families the brothers all had different characters. Each had a different inner spiritual awareness. The eldest brother, John, didn't know which career to follow. His parents advised him to study for a career in accountancy because he had a natural ability to work with figures. Many years later he was earning a modest income as an accountant. The youngest brother, Sam, did well in his exam grades at school and college. He had no idea what work he wanted to do for a work career, but he had a strong work ethic and managed to earn an income as a went through life, but with several different career changes. The middle brother, Richard, didn't do particularly well in his school and college exams. Not that he wasn't intelligent. It was just that studying didn't interest him. What he did have was an inner vision that someday he would be a successful builder and property developer. With tunnel vision and determination to keep to his vision he did study for builders' qualifications. After working as an apprentice whilst he learnt his trade, he went on to establish his own building company. He kept the inner drive and determination to achieving his vision which was now to become successful with his building and property development company. He eventually became a wealthy man, and his company employed a huge number of people as it acquired new housing and office development contracts. Richard was the most successful of his brothers simply because he kept to his tunnel vision end goal, knowing exactly what he wanted to achieve in life.

Our Guardian Angels will help us to achieve our dreams, if they are realistic. Often, our inner visions are seeded in our Life Plan that was set before we were born. An important lesson is that Heaven will help us achieve our goals, our visions, if they are good and do not hurt others. We should keep to our visions with a determination to not be knocked off course because that makes it easier for Heaven to put things in place to help us along the way.

Help from the Angels

The following true account is interesting in the way that a life can be dramatically changed by working with our Guardian Angels in spiritually analysing a person's life in recent years to bring about a much brighter and positive future:

I was called to a home in Hull to give Angel message readings, to a bunch of family and friends who had booked me. Halfway through the evening I was invited into a room to read for a lady in her late sixties. I had met these friends gathered in the lounge, and then one at a time walked through to the kitchen/diner to give each a private reading. The room this lady was sat in was in between the lounge and kitchen. It was reasonably big, decorated in the flowery wallpaper so popular in the 1970s. This was the year 2006. I noticed that there was no window in the room, but it was bright and clean. She looked happy, but as I started to give her a reading, I felt very much that her life was on hold. I immediately was given a vision of a man with her in spirit who I knew was her husband. I told her this, she nodded to confirm, when I was then given a picture of a scene of a hospital bed. The same man was laid there with full life support systems attached. A doctor was in this scene looking past me at the lady I was with, asking her permission to switch off the life support. The doctor was telling her that there was nothing more the medical professionals could do. Her husband was technically brain dead, but his body was being kept alive by the machines. I gently told the lady what I was seeing. She remained calm and told me that her husband had died six years earlier. The doctor had indeed asked her permission to switch off the life support. She couldn't say yes, so went for a walk around the local streets. She had then walked back into the ward still unable to bring herself to give permission. Suddenly she just came out with the words necessary, giving permission for the life support to be switched off. The lady had remained calm whilst she told me all of this. She then became quite emotional, and said, "I murdered him. I murdered him. I have locked myself away in this room for the past six years. I haven't been out. I am looked after by my family, but I won't go out. I killed my husband." Her emotional outburst shocked me, but only momentarily. I was instantly taken back to the hospital ward. I had a bird's-eye view of her returning after her walk. I could see and hear her asking for the doctor, still undecided what to do, when suddenly her husband appeared, stood alongside her in spirit whispering in her ear "Switch off the life support. I am ok, I am free of my wrecked body, please tell him you give your permission, my love". The vision disappeared and I sat facing this emotionally distraught lady sat in front of me. I told her what I had just seen. I told her that her husband had not really been lying there in the hospital bed but was stood alongside her in spirit asking her to tell the doctor to switch off the life support.

The visions from my Guardian Angel closed as I sat opposite this lady. She slowly lifted her drooping head and stared at me eye to eye. Then a smile appeared. "You couldn't have known all of this. I now believe that my husband still exists. I did the right thing. I made the right decision."

I was then ushered out of her room to give another reading in the kitchen to a friend who had been waiting. At the end of the evening, I walked into the lounge to say goodbye to everyone. The air of excitement was electrifying. A middle-aged lady who must have been the daughter said, "Mum has told us she is no longer grieving, she is no longer blaming herself for Dad's death. She wants to get her life going again. Her first request is that I take her out shopping tomorrow. Thank you for what you have done. You have no idea what a miracle it is to see Mum wanting to live her life again." I said goodnight, feeling very much that something much bigger than me was at work. I can't perform miracles but overwhelmingly felt humbled to be a part of something so life changing.

What we may become will be shaped by our future experience

LIFE GUIDE

Our Life Guide is a part of our Life Plan and shows how people should live their lives to gain a better place in Heaven.

Most ordinary people go to Heaven at the end of physical life. We can earn a "Better Place" in Heaven if we live our lives in a certain way.

When we say, "Better Place", then for all of us "Heaven" is a beautiful place to be. However, we are still shown the mistakes we made, and shown where we hurt others. Hurting others may have been either psychological hurt, or physical harm that we caused. Even the mostly good and caring people can accidentally or unintentionally hurt others at times, for such is the difficulty in living in our world. However, it seems to be that deliberate hurt is the most serious wrongdoing.

If we were guilty of deliberate hurt, pain, and harm against others in our life then this may be presented before us by Wise Beings in Heaven, who want us to learn. They can, if they so decide, make us intensely aware of how the hurt we caused impacted on our victims.

In First Heaven we are also shown the good things that we did, the help and care we gave to our families, and others, and our care for animals and nature.

So, First Heaven is as beautiful and loving as you might expect, and a place for learning, and reflection on the life we just had.

My research shows absolutely that there is a God or "Source" of infinite intelligence, unconditional love, but you do not have to believe. You can live through a lifetime as a non-believer, and your place in the spiritual realm of Heaven is still waiting for you. You do not have to earn it, although you will be side-tracked if you are truly evil.

My research shows that the physical universe, and all of life and nature were deliberately created. Again, you do not have to believe this. It doesn't matter if you are a sceptic, or total non-believer.

My research shows that Evolution also took place. Similar forms of life in plants and animals did adapt through the laws of survival, changing to fit the climate, habitat and food sources of where they lived.

Evolution has also seen deliberate intervention at specific points in time by those that worked in the Creator's purpose to create new life and bring about totally new species.

Whatever we do in life, however we live our lives, the most important rule of living is to be caring and loving of others, of animals, of nature and of our planet.

Soulmates

The term "Soulmate" describes a spiritual connection between two people that precedes this life. We may meet our soulmates in this life, and we may have more than one.

Often our friends and family may not be spiritual soulmates.

When we do meet a soulmate there is an instant understanding between one another. There is a feeling of having a spiritual connection, and both of you feeling the same way, and being on the same level in a way that words cannot describe. This doesn't mean that such a person will be a partner to us in life, for often

soulmates meet and then move on in separate directions.
The most intense soulmate relationship is where such a person is a partner or family member
Our Soulmates preceded our life, for we were with them in Heaven before we were born. Meeting a soulmate can be an important event in our Life-Plan. If it is, then our Guardian Angels will enable this, by putting a series of events in place in our lives to make our meeting with our soulmate just happen!

Angelic People

We should judge people by their actions, rather than what they say they might do.

Often, people may promise to help others, and promise to care, but their words never become actions.

There are some people who just "Get on" with helping others in spiritual love and care. They are so dedicated and caring towards others that they almost seem Angelic.

Our research has discovered that people who show spiritual love, and physically help and care for others often have an Angel working closely with them.

In everyday life our Guardian Angel stands back from us, and helps us, when necessary, provided that we do not block our Angel through our self-centred Free Will.

When we are truly doing something that is spiritually loving and caring towards others then our Guardian Angel comes closer to help us and pass into us spiritual energies of the right kind. If we are trying to help someone who is sick, then our Guardian Angel will channel healing energies through us.

If our heart is pure, and we are dedicated in helping others, then sometimes our Angel will meld with us to become one with us. Such people may feel energised in body and in purpose. Others looking on may describe that person as "An Angel" because of their self-sacrifice and care for others.

It is not just in helping people that our Angels work. They also work through people who actively help and care for animals, for nature, and for the environment of planet Earth.

HEAVEN

Guardian Angels do not abandon us when our life is at an
end. They work hard to care and comfort us towards the end
of life, and then reveal themselves to us when we leave our
physical body. We pass into a most beautiful light, and then
find ourselves moving through a portal towards the other side
of life. We move towards a place that I call "First Heaven". This
is a place where most ordinary, and basically good people pass
across to at the end of life's days in the physical. Most people do
not have to earn their place in the Spiritual Realm of Heaven.
Our main Guardian Angel meets us at the gateway to Heaven
and guides us forward into the realms of Heaven.
There are other Heavens, but I feel it important to tell the world
about First Heaven, because it is the place most ordinary people
without strong religious beliefs go to after so called "death". If
you have your own religious faith, then your religion will teach
you about their Heaven.
First Heaven is surprisingly solid and much more real than the
physical world around us. There are beautiful valleys, rivers,
trees, and flowers in radiant bloom of most vivid colours. We
are free of pain, and emotional suffering. We may realise that
First Heaven is a familiar place like going home. We were there
before we were born. We may be given a beautiful garden to rest.
We may be given a place similar to our home to rest and feel at

ease whilst we adjust to our new spiritual state, now free of our physical body with all its pain.

Loved ones who have passed before us may wait for us there, and we can find the joy of being re-united with them.

First Heaven is a "Gateway" to the further Heavens. For those with their own religious faiths then there are other "Gateways" that are described and taught by their faith.

People who were evil in life do not go to First Heaven but are side-tracked elsewhere.

In First Heaven

The Light above us is a "Sky" of gentle white light, yet whiter than any shade of white you can imagine. There is a "One" whom people may call "God", "The Source", "The Creator".

The "Oneness" of the universe, of all spiritual beings, is felt very strongly in First Heaven, a place of unconditional love. We are loved for who we are, no matter what our faults. Love is the air we breathe.

In First Heaven we can appear as we did in life with our human body. Our true self is an orb of Light and Conscious Energy, so we can also appear as that.

Communication in First Heaven is by pure thought. We instantly know what is being communicated to us, and we can talk/communicate through our thoughts.

In First Heaven we can rest if our soul needs to build up energy again after a hard life. We can also be busy and continue learning.

We very much see and are accompanied by the "Guardian Angels" who helped us through life, and other Higher Angelic Beings.

From First Heaven our Guardian Angels may help us look-on at those whom we love that are still in life. We can be seen by those with a gift of clairvoyance. We are not "Ghosts" when we are in First Heaven. Ghosts are something different.

LIFE REVIEW

We are given a "Life Review" in First Heaven. This is done in a loving way to see what we achieved, or to examine where we went wrong. Our lives are given to us for "Adventure", "Experience" and "Learning". The end goal is to hopefully become less self-centred, and more caring, loving and giving to others. This leads to spiritual growth.

We are shown in a loving way the mistakes and harm we may have caused to hurt others in life. We are also shown our achievements.

From this we can see that the most important lesson whilst still in life is to be loving and caring towards other people, and towards animals, nature, all of life, and the planet we live on.

Should we have done wrong it is a good idea to think about it now whilst in life, and to contemplate the errors we made. If we can try to make amends by becoming more loving and caring, this is much better than not bothering until we pass across to First Heaven.

Have you ever had a moment in your life where you could see your life clearly?

Have you ever thought: "What regrets will I carry at the end of my life? What will I wish I had done?"

A brief moment in time when we can stop in our busy lives and experience a moment of wonderful, intense clear thinking!

We may suddenly see one thing or several things that we should start to do. Things that will be positive experiences in our life that we never had time to do.

You see, in Heaven we can look back on our lives and review what we did. Heaven is a beautiful place, full of love. However, it is in this life where we can find adventure and raw experience. It is in this life that we can write a new page of our life diary each new day.

Our Guardian Angel may get through to us in moments of clear thinking, showing us things that we could be doing to maximise our life fulfilment. We should grasp these special moments with an intensity of purpose and bring changes into our life as soon as possible!

Past Lives

As a human soul we were at some point in the distant past born out of the Spiritual Oneness of the Source of all Conscious Energy.
The Spiritual Dimension is a very real dimension. It is our true home. Our soul, the person whom we are, is made of conscious energy, and so the Spiritual Dimension of Heaven is our familiar home from where we came, and to where we return after each life.
I believe that soul energy has been around throughout infinity, and yet gives birth to new individual souls who are given many lives in the physical universe. For most of us the recurring lives are on Earth as human beings.

The reason for human beings having many lives seems to be complex but driven by some very simple principles. These are:
To have adventure and experience.

To gain an identity. In Heaven we are an individual soul, living with other souls, and the air that we breathe is unconditional love. On Earth we are given a name, an identity, and we carve out our own path of success or failure.

The most important reason for our life is to learn to love and care for others, and for animals and nature. This is the only way that we will spiritually grow. People who have no empathy, no consideration for others will not spiritually grow, and will stay at the same soul level, or even go back to an earlier level of soul development if they have been bad to others whilst in life.

We might have started our first life 100,000 years ago and lived through many lives. Once we are at a sufficient stage in our spiritual development, we will reach a point where we don't have to go back into a life again. We will have other work to do in the Spiritual Realm.

Many of us will have started our life journey as recent as several hundred years ago. We will still have many future lives to come. The time between lives can be several hundred years, or we can be reborn as frequent as twice per century. Many souls in Heaven have wanted to be back in life through the latter part of the 20th century, and early 21st century due to the different experience that science and technology has brought about. They all want the experience of travel by car and plane, computers, TV, mobile phones, and a less physical struggle compared with the primitive rural lives they might have had in the past. That is why there are over seven billion people alive today.

An interesting thing can be pointed out: Those who don't care about the planet and climate change don't realise that future generations will probably include a reincarnated life for them, so they will also suffer as reborn souls.

There are many true accounts of readings that I have given concerning how our past lives affect our present life.

Kelly (not her real name) came to me for an Angel message reading. Without her saying anything I was immediately given a message from the Angels that she had at least three long-term relationships that had ended badly. I also could see that she presently didn't have a close relationship.

Kelly immediately responded by saying "You are correct. Why does this always happen to me? Why can't I have a long-term, happy relationship?"

I added to my reading by seeing that her first relationship by marriage was very brutal. She had been subject to mental and physical abuse. She confirmed that, and almost broke down in tears.

I knew I had to get to the cause of these recurring relationship problems, and I sensed the Angels giving me visions on her immediate past life. I saw that she had been a woman (sometimes we have different genders in different lives), and that she had been married happily for over forty years. Her marriage in this past life was full of love, and she had been a mother to several children. I then saw a vision of her husband in this past life and compared it with the vision of her three failed relationships in this life. That's the answer! In this life she had instinctively been attracted to men with similar appearance, similar physical qualities to her husband in the past lives. This instinctive attraction had over-ridden the personality problems of her three failed relationships who had all treated her badly and each hurt her in their own way.

I told her the conclusions that this Life Plan reading had given. She sat there for a minute, saying nothing, and absorbing what I had said. "You are right," she said. "It all makes sense!"

I advised her to look at the personal, character qualities of any future partner. Some weeks later I saw her again. She is now in another relationship with a man she says has a pleasant character and is genuinely caring. She seems really happy.

*Our Life Plan was determined in
Heaven before we were born.*

We will emerge from a life on Earth back in our familiar home
of Heaven having been shaped by our most recent life, and still
carrying our experiences from previous lives.

We will have gained yet another identity, a new name, in our last
life. We will need a period of adjustment, a period of orientation
now we are back in the spiritual realm of Heaven.

Most souls go to a place that I name "First Heaven". I have already
gone into further detail of First Heaven elsewhere in this book,
but it is best described as a place with similarities to Earth.
There are beautiful flowers, trees, and all of nature resplendent
in a landscape of valleys, vivid green grass, streams, and even
houses. People may appear as they did in life, usually in middle
age or younger. Our Guardian Angel accompanies us during this
time, when we are also given a Life Review to see our life, almost
like a video. During the Life Review will we see the good things
that we did, our mistakes, and the hurt we may have caused
others.

It also happens that in addition to adventure and experience
during our physical life we are also measured on our ability to
love and care for others, including all of life in animals and
nature.

In First Heaven we can look-on at loved ones who are still
alive in the physical. This is when people, such as myself, can
make a connection and bring messages. Such connection is via
Guardian Angels. The word Angel interprets as "Messenger".

After a long period of time in First Heaven (although there is no
such thing as time across there, only the moment of "Now"), we
move on towards further learning and experience in other areas
of Heaven. We will re-unite with our true soulmates who were
born as a soul at the same time as ourselves. We may talk to each

other to share our individual experiences in our lives on Earth. We may have met at least one of our soulmates in life, been a friend with one of them, or even shared a life as a partner or family member with a soulmate.

At some point we will be encouraged to move forward and agree to being born again into another life as a human being. This isn't forced on us, especially if our previous life was painful or traumatic. Our soul is given a chance to rest and rebuild our soul energy.

Before we go into a new life our Life Plan is drawn up by our Guardian Angel, together with other wise beings. These beings are like people, but spiritual beings who have lived through many lives and are now teachers.

Our Life Plan will address our character deficits from a perspective of developing our soul to be more loving and caring of others whilst in life. Our Life Plan can build-in the interests we may wish to develop, the work we might do, and the people we are destined to meet.

Life Plans will always include Life Challenges which are never easy but are not meant to cause personal suffering.

Free Will is destined to influence our day-to-day decisions, yet the major events and people we are destined to meet on our Life Plan will still happen, no matter what our free will decisions do to our lives.

Some souls volunteer for a life where they will have some physical disability, or a particularly tough life. This is because our souls learn more rapidly and spiritually develop to a higher level through hardship and struggle. If we are still able to be caring and loving towards others when our life is tough then we are truly spiritually bigger and stronger, and that's what Heaven seems to want of us.

LIFE PLAN MESSAGES

Much of our life up to now, our present, and our future, was planned-out in Heaven before we were born.

With messages and visions from my Guardian Angel I scan the past lives of a person, and then move on to visions of the time in Heaven when their Life Plan for this life was being worked out and drawn up.

I'll give you a true example:

Richard came to me for a Life Plan reading. He had been through a divorce and was concerned for his children so shared custody with his ex-wife.

He was in some ways lonely, and needed to find a new friendship, a new partner, but his divorce had meant giving his home up to his ex-wife, and short of money for moving on, and no time for finding new friends.

I started by seeing if the Angels would give me visions of his past lives. When I work with the Angels in this way, I mainly pick up feelings of how a person was in past lives. I could see he had been quite selfish in his past lives and had only thought about his own needs. This had meant that others around him had been psychologically hurt by his lack of care.

Then came the Life Review whilst in Heaven before his present life. I could see that being selfish had held back his spiritual growth. He had agreed with the wise ones who put together his Life Plan that he would try to be more caring of others next time. I was then given visions of his life up to now. I could see that he had clashed with his ex-wife because she was and is very self-centred. He wanted to be there for his children in sharing custody. He seemed determined to work hard at being genuinely caring, not putting himself first.

I explained the Angel messages to him, and he agreed with the findings.

I further explained that he was going through a period of his life when the interests of the children, and the needs of the children to still have a caring father, were more important than his own personal wishes, and he agreed.

Looking to the future for him I could see a vision of a future partner, an improved financial position and new home. The timeline of the vision coming to fruition was, however, several years hence. He said he was happy at that. He felt justified in his present lifestyle of some self-sacrifice for the benefit of his children and was so impressed at the accuracy of the reading that he felt he could now feel less anxious about his present life. I saw him several times, and each time he felt he was becoming spiritually calmer, stronger and wiser, and that he was less depressed and coping with everyday life much better.

What about things that happen to people to prevent life fulfilment?

Wars, accidents, pandemics, and other events that lead to human severe suffering are not usually on a person's Life Plan. Lives cut short by such tragedies see a soul return to Heaven earlier than planned.

The first process in Heaven is to give a soul rest, counselling, and a chance to rejuvenate their soul energies. A Life Plan can be picked up again, perhaps modified, and made ready for a new life once a person feels ready to enter another life.
Heaven is always viewed as a safe retreat for us, a familiar home where we truly belong. However, the lack of any memory of Heaven, combined with the cold, painful hardships of life leave us as human beings reluctant to accept that those in Heaven exist, let alone truly love us.
Also, many people have a terrific passion for life, and work hard towards achieving success in education, sport, music, art, and business. In addition, many people build up a family, and life seems at its most harsh when any tragedy strikes.

The Life Challenges that are set for us on our Life Plan are not life tragedies. Also, no matter whom we are as a soul our Life Plan may be severely restricted by others around. We may care for someone with a disability for many years and put our own dreams aside. This is where we surrender our free will to help others. This is of course spiritually positive and will help our continued soul development.

We may live in a society that restricts personal freedoms, or we might find ourselves poor in an affluent society where money rules. Both are examples of how our Life Plan might not attain fulfilment.

It is when I am giving a person details of their current and past life situation that I often find that they want to know more about what the future holds for them.

I can move into a Life Plan reading seamlessly, and very quickly look at their past life. I ask my Guardian Angel specific questions, in my mind thoughts, concerning the Life Plan of my client. My Guardian Angel works with the Angels that accompany my client.

The questions I ask can typically include: Is the unfair and difficult time in my client's life now at an end? What better future can my client have? What are the hopes and dreams of my client, and will these be achieved in the future?

At this point on the reading assessment, I can explain to the client all that I have been given in clairvoyant messages and visions. I then "Block" any unwanted things that could happen in my client's future should he or she simply carry on as they are with life. I then explain to the client the positive things that will come into their life, and as I explain the good things, such as a new friend, a new job or career, a new home, or perhaps fulfilment in sport, art, or music, I can see that a process is underway of changing their future Life Path for the better.

The following is a true case:

Linda came to see me. I could see her deceased mother in spirit. The love bond between them was strong and I brought through a lot of information from her deceased mother, including a message to not feel guilty for not being by her side when she unexpectedly passed. This message was received emotionally by Linda who was overjoyed to have re-united with her mother for those few minutes. I might have ended the reading there, but I was seeing visions of her life and that she wasn't completely happy. She was happily married with two children but couldn't understand why she felt deep-down unhappy.

I reviewed her past life where I picked-up that she had been a musician, playing the piano, and her best friend in her previous life, a female, had been one of her soulmates who was also a musician. I reviewed her life up to now, and she had money, a happy family, everything most people would want, but hadn't given herself any space for her own interests, the main one of which was music.

I then asked for visions of her Life Plan. I could see that if she took up music as a hobby and took time to learn a musical instrument then she would find long-term fulfilment and she would also meet her soulmate again, and a close friendship would happen.

Linda was amazed at the revelations from her Angel messages Life Plan reading, and excited to be on a new path of life fulfilment, now very determined to allow herself time for her own passion in music.

CHAPTER THIRTEEN

Past Lives

When I am giving an Angel messages reading, I am often given visions of future positive events. These are always impressive, but I personally would often feel that I could help people more. Angel readings are meant to help people move forward with their lives in a positive way.
I always sense other underlying factors at play in a person's past, present, and future life. Finding out what these factors are can help give a much clearer view of our individual futures.
When giving someone a reading I often see that there could be a choice of futures. I needed to know what clairvoyant guidance I could give someone to help them live a more positive, happier and fulfilling future.

I was a Christian until aged fifty-five years. I thought that the messages and spiritual visions from the Angels were religious experiences, even though many years of spiritual research were revealing a different picture to the teachings of my faith. Most Christian faiths disapprove of anyone having visions, and I eventually had to be sincere to myself in quietly stepping down from my Christian work which at that time was as a trainee Methodist preacher.
I now believe that we all have experienced many past lives. Christian beliefs are in our one life only, and to strive towards

salvation through our beliefs, actions and deeds in this life.

Although I now know that we, as an eternal soul, have many lives, I am still passionate about living this life as if it were the only life that we have.

Past Lives can sometimes be identified through a personal hypnotherapy consultation.

Some clairvoyants, including myself, can pick up on a person's immediate past life, and even some previous past lives.

Our past lives have helped make us into the person we are in this life and continue to influence our present life in many ways.

Inner feelings that we can't explain could be caused by a previous past life.

The following is a true account, but with the person's name changed.

I gave Katie an Angel messages reading. I had never met her before, and she appeared to be around the age of sixty years. I immediately felt the pain of a recently broken relationship, and she confirmed that as being correct.

I asked her to say nothing and told her that I could see that she has three adult children, and that the father was from an earlier relationship break-up.

I was given a vision of a partner in spirit, with her, and he was very apologetic concerning his behaviour in the latter part of their relationship.

Katie confirmed that she had been through three marriages, and that all three husbands had turned to drinking excess alcohol, and became selfish, and aggressive. She had to pull away from each of the marriages.

"Why does this always happen to me!" came as an outburst from Katie.

The partner who had died was with her in spirit, and confirmed that he had been her second husband, and after 14 years of happy marriage had suffered a major personality change after becoming an alcoholic.

He was sorry for his selfish behaviour. I passed this message on to Katie, and she then told me that her marriage with him had been the "Best".

I couldn't explain "Why this is always happening to her" in an immediate spiritual assessment.

However, my Guardian Angel started to give me visions of Katie's past life. She had been happily married in her past life, and I began to see that in her present life she had been attracted to men with similar looks to her husband in her past life. She had just "Felt" that a prospective partner was right for her, based on his looks, not knowing why, and disregarding a future partner's character defects.

Being a different gender in a past life can be an explanation for our feelings in this life

The following is a true account, but with her name changed.

Linda, age mid-twenties, came to see me for an Angel messages reading. She was, and is, openly a lesbian, and admitted that her true feelings had emerged after having some unpleasant relationships with men in her teenage years.

Linda had a massive anger problem and felt that she couldn't conform with school and education when younger and was now unemployed and unable to focus on a career.

She was looking for a loving relationship with another woman, but as yet was unable to find true happiness.

At first the Angel messages for her gave nothing concerning her personal difficulties, only that her grandfather gave some simple messages.

Suddenly, my Guardian Angel gave me a vision of a young man, aged nineteen years, in a battle. It was World War Two, and he was fighting alongside his comrades when they were hit by an artillery shell. The first experience he had was of his soul being thrown out of his body, and himself in spirit being pulled into the Light of Heaven.

We leave anger and stress behind before we reach Heaven. Even so, his regret at having his life cut short of not experiencing a long and loving relationship with a girlfriend carried in his memory.

Once reborn into a new life in the 1990s, as a female, named Linda, he had lost his memory of his immediate past life. However, the anger re-emerged, and his search for a loving female relationship eventually started to dominate him, now as Linda.

Upon communicating this vision to Linda, she immediately felt that at last there was an explanation for her anger, and for not being interested in a career. She felt that she had at last realised who she was and is. She will continue looking for a happy, loving, lesbian relationship, and hopefully find some employment career, now knowing how her past life has affected her present life in such a big way.

As we progress through many lives we naturally want to ask: "Why do we have lots of lives?
Living lives for the adventure and experience are certainly some of the main reasons.

Those in Heaven see the Grand Purpose of our lives as becoming more caring and loving towards others, animals, nature, and our beautiful planet, and being less self-centred.

It would seem as though younger souls are naturally more self-centred, and more mature souls become more loving and caring to others.

I have considered this carefully in my research over many years and come to the conclusion that for Heaven to survive, those souls dwelling there must be loving and caring to each other. It's a feeling of Oneness.

This feeling of Oneness is so strong in Heaven that as we become aware of how we hurt others, and hurt nature, then we start to realise that we are equally hurting ourselves.

Planet Earth has many younger souls. This is self-evident in self-centred behaviour, and lack of empathy towards others, that is widespread.

Mature souls are more loving and caring. They may sacrifice many of their own worldly pleasures to help others, and nature.

So, our present and future life is being determined by our spiritual progress. This can be identified clairvoyantly.

Between Lives – Life Review

At the end of each life our soul, the person that we may call "I" or "Me", leaves our physical body, and returns home to Heaven.

After many years of giving Angel message readings, I realise that we carry across there not only our character, but also our memories.

When reading to connect with someone who suffered from dementia, I find that spiritually retained memories only go as recent as immediately prior to the onset of their dementia.

We do not carry serious emotions, stress, anger, worry, or sorrow across with us. We leave these behind as we find ourselves entering the spiritual realm of pure, unconditional love.

When we leave our physical body, we will find ourselves seeing our Guardian Angel, probably for the first time. Our Guardian Angel will appear as a person, but radiant with soul energy. We will not feel afraid, but instinctively know that this is a Being of love.

Most people, most souls, pass across to Heaven after their physical life is at an end.

I call this place "First Heaven" because it is the first place we travel to.

First Heaven is very real and solid. The immense beauty and vivid colours are beyond description.

There are fields, trees, flowers, rivers and lakes. There may also be homes, similar to a home where a soul may have lived on Earth.

I describe First Heaven in more detail elsewhere in this book. However, we will have many things to do. These include re-uniting with our soulmates, a Life Review, looking at our Life Lessons and spending time with Wise Beings in the Afterlife who will assess our spiritual progress.

Planning our next life

Our next life is planned in Heaven before we are reborn. We will be aware of our future Life Plan and know the reasons why our future life will hold Life Lessons.

When we are reborn, the conscious memory of our time in Heaven is deliberately erased. However, our Guardian Angels know our Life Plan, and by becoming more aware of our Guardian Angels, and how they communicate through our feelings, we can be more in touch with understanding the reasons for our life experience in the past and present and obtain a glimpse of our future Life Plan events yet to happen.

Working with my Guardian Angel, I can pick up messages and visions of our future Life Plan events clairvoyantly.

Past Life behaviour will determine some of our present life experiences

Whilst in Heaven we will at some point experience a Life Review. This usually happens soon after our passing.

Our Life Review is in the presence of our Guardian Angel, and Higher Spiritual Beings, often appearing in human form.

A lot of emphasis is given on how much we helped others in our lives. This is classed as good and positive.

In situations where we were totally self-centred in our behaviour towards others, these situations will be brought to our attention. If we were lacking in empathy, and in situations where we deliberately hurt others emotionally or physically, then this is looked on as bad behaviour. We can be shown life situations in our life that has passed as if reliving them in real time, but this time feeling the hurt we may have caused.

How are we punished for bad behaviour?
Punishment isn't the correct way of describing the outcome of our bad behaviour. Heaven is a place of unconditional love and safety for all who make it there, and most souls do reach Heaven successfully.

After our Life Review, there is a realisation at a spiritual level of shared responsibility for each other. A feeling of "Oneness" of all souls, and that if we hurt another soul, we are also hurting ourselves.

We eventually will volunteer for another life where we might agree to be a victim of someone who treats us badly, just as we hurt others in the past. This would be to give us an experience where we can learn. Our souls often grow more quickly in positive ways during hard times in life.

If we can endure our own difficult life, and yet still be caring towards others, then we are truly growing spiritually.

So, it can be seen that our past lives, followed by our Life Plan mapped out in Heaven, would have had a significant role to play in our current life. This often explains why some people's lives seem to have been harder than others.

The good news is that if we sense our Guardian Angel we can learn to identify "Life challenges" set before we were born.

For all of us, learning to be closer to our Guardian Angels can help us "Feel" that we know our Life challenges.

Can the Life challenges be avoided in the future and a person's life changed for the better? ***Absolutely, yes!***

Our future after this life – will be affected by our behaviour in this life

CHAPTER FOURTEEN

LIFE AS A PERSON SEEING ANGELS

This chapter is written to explain further what I see and experience.

There is no scientific evidence of the eternal spiritual soul that we all are and have. It is the person inside whom we call "I" or "Me". That person inside has an eternal existence beyond our physical life.

Everything spiritual, including our soul, is of another dimension. That is why physical science cannot detect our soul and cannot detect Heaven.

Within ourselves, we are a soul of conscious, intelligent energy made of the same stuff as the energies of Heaven. Heaven is our true familiar home where we came from, and to where we return.

The human brain is most amazing. The brain has within the ability to link and meld with our soul energy. The neurons firing within the brain create energies that communicate with our soul energy so perfectly that we feel as one with our human body born into the physical world of Earth. The brain is a link with both the dimension of Heaven and Earth. Perhaps future discoveries of how this link works might provide some scientific evidence of the spiritual dimension.

What do I experience as a person Sensing Angels?
Well, firstly I try to ground myself in everyday life. I am a qualified accountant and have always worked hard in my career. I have hobbies and interests, and a passion for my main interest – music.

Sending Angels is something that I can switch-on when my mind turns to it.

When I am giving someone a reading, I sense their Guardian Angel communicating with my Guardian Angel. It is they who enable the readings to happen. I am given visions as images of people who have passed, of scenes in someone's life, of landscapes, homes, cars, and almost anything. The visions are always of relevance to the person I am helping through the reading. I also receive information, either as a sudden voice when I am given a name, or a sudden "knowingness".

What I do find consistently is that the readings only occur where there is a bond of love, family, or friendship, between the person in front of me and the person in spirit.

Throughout my life I have also been given visions of other things:

I can see across to Heaven.
The place I see is a place I call "First Heaven". This is because this is the first place we go to after we pass across from our physical life.

I can see people who are in spirit where there is a love or friendship connection.

I can receive messages via my Guardian Angel in the form of visions, and messages as a voice or "Sudden knowingness".

I can see the Guardian Angels of people and I can communicate with them.

I can see that Angels respond to our prayers to God. The Angels work on the instructions and in the purpose of God.

I can see Angels bringing healing to people. I can see the different colours of the energies Angels channel when bringing healing. I can help people myself in channelling healing from the Angels.

I can see Life Plans, and some of a person's future. The future is also determined by our free will.

I can see Angels working in nature.

I can see, feel, and know the meaning of life.

As we learn to sense Angels, we witness them helping people in many ways.

Angels help all of us as we near the end of life, and when we pass across to Heaven.

I have had an account from a nurse who has worked in the resuscitation ward of hospital. She informed me that whenever she saw an Angel at the bed head of a patient, she knew the patient was more likely to die. The doctors and her would inevitably have a more difficult time, but often still saved the life of such patients.

Angels may bring healing. A prayer to God can bring direct healing help through the Angels and help by bringing professional medical attention.

Angels help behind the scenes to provide our basic needs of food, clothing, a friend to talk to.

What do you really want out of life? What do you need most to achieve fulfilment? Well. The Angels won't help you win the lottery, but they can offer a tremendous amount of help in achieving our goals, and fulfilment in life. What do we need to do? Well, the starting point is simply to be open-minded to a belief in Angels!

LIFE CHANGING EXPERIENCES

Life- changing experiences are quiet, personal ones. Earlier in the book I described how I felt a Guardian Angel with me when I was near death in hospital with asthma. However, as I grew older, into my teens, as with any normal teenager my mind forgot about spiritual experiences from my infancy. My subsequent life-changing experiences were quiet, personal ones. I wasn't suddenly going to change the world overnight by bringing to the world my vision, and a new way of life. No, the world doesn't change. Life hopefully continues. We should count each day as a blessing. We should think of the things we have in this life and be thankful. We should try not to become too depressed or consume ourselves with jealousy because of things we don't have. Earlier in the book I described a very real experience of a vision and a spiritual journey given to me by an Archangel on 1[st]May, 1999. Over the weeks and months following my journey into Heaven I experienced visions of Light many times. I still do, to this day. When the moments are more intense, I see the face of the Heavenly Being. His eyes always draw my attention. They have depths of infinite wisdom, understanding and unconditional love. Immediately after my journey to Heaven I knew I was being prepared to do some kind of spiritual work to help others. I could ask in my thoughts almost any question about the meaning of life, and the answer would be given to me. I was on a rapid learning curve. I learnt the power of prayer, and that non selfish prayers to God are listened to and answered, but not always with the answer we want!

The big negative is that life-changing experiences don't change the world around you. I still had to work for a living. I had family to keep, a mortgage to pay, and couldn't just drop everything for some spiritual adventure. I still struggled with all the pain and difficulties of normal life.

I broached the subject of spiritual experiences with friends. The boredom factor quickly set in whenever I tried to discuss my experience with my good friends who were normal mates. We enjoyed a good laugh and sharing each other's problems. If I began to talk about what had happened, it just seemed weird to them.

I then had this idea that surely some people who went to Church must be drawn to religion because they had similar spiritual experiences. I started attending a fundamentalist Christian Church, but after several months I realised I couldn't have been more wrong. I found out that the Holy Scripture says that the devil appears as an angel of light. Anyone who spoke of seeing angels was condemned for seeing the devil. It seems that religious miracles are with some faiths confined to two thousand years ago, and not permitted since. What about my spiritual gift of discernment between good and evil? In my visions I can discern between visions from Heaven, and the evil antics of demons, and negative energies. Holy Scripture teaches us about spiritual gifts as being "Fruits of the spirit". Every one of us has a gift, a talent, and discernment is a gift I have been granted. Why would I be criticised for simply being honest and truthful? We are all different. We should make the most of the talents and abilities. Also, we should not dwell on the gifts that we don't have but others do.

However, I didn't want condemnation by religious fundamentalists, so I told myself I wasn't going to allow myself to see ghosts. I wanted to try to use my spiritual gifts through normal channels, restricting myself in what I said and did, and conforming to Christian teachings. I moved to join another less fundamental Church and spent four years training to be a Christian preacher.

During those four years I was judged as a good preacher. I kept strictly to the Church doctrine and had a ready gift when it came to what is called "Exegesis". This is where we read a passage from Scripture and interpret the relevance in today's modern world. I wrote spiritual poetry, always including one of my poems in a service. During my four years preaching I led over one hundred services. These were often commented on as being services with an atmosphere of healing. I would even get letters from members of the congregation commenting on how my service had given them a sensation of healing, even though I deliberately kept the services formal. The services were sometimes recorded and made available at the local hospital for patients to hear. My spiritual poetry received local acclaim, and I gave poetry readings on local radio, and was privileged to read my poems at events within the region.

The visions, however, kept appearing. I remember trying to console a bereaved widow in a Christian way, seeing clearly her husband stood with her, yet unable to comment or give her a message. Christian teachings in my Church were that the only people who went to Heaven were those who had been Baptised, accepted Jesus Christ as their Lord and Saviour, and led an active Christian Life within the Church, living a life of repentance and worship.

Conversations with Church Ministers, Vicars, Priests, and Pastors seemed to give no indication that they could see the things I was seeing. I felt sad at Vicars leading funerals for non-Christians with words indicating that the deceased would be in Heaven. Yet I knew the teachings of their faith meant they couldn't truly believe that the deceased had passed across to everlasting life in Heaven. After four years I quietly stood down from preaching. I believed in the work I had been doing as a preacher. Churches do teach people there is a God, and how we should live good lives. Churches also teach us to respect God, to repent for our mistakes, and live this life as if it were our only chance to get to Heaven. I have since learnt we have many lives, but that doesn't mean that this very life we are in now shouldn't be lived to the utmost in our caring for others, for nature, and the planet so that we may spiritually grow.

I was a Christian by religion, but I could no longer hold back the bigger picture and the work I had to do, however controversial. My true clairvoyant work was about to begin.............

BEING SPIRITUALLY AWARE

WE DON'T CHANGE IMMEDIATELY. A door to spiritual awareness is within each one of us. In many it remains closed throughout life. For some the door can be gradually opened.

It was the year 1966. I was age sixteen and a screeching of tyres, together with the roaring sound of an engine at maximum revs filled my ears. I was sat passenger in my mate's Mini 850cc as he drove it as if he were driving a rally car around the bends of the country roads surrounding our home village of Silsden in the Yorkshire Dales. He was seventeen and had just passed his driving test. The car had been acquired by my mate for next to nothing. I didn't ask if it was taxed, insured and properly serviced. After half an hour of clinging onto the seat just wishing I was driving and wishing I could drive like him we stopped outside of his house. The car looked worse for wear with shabby paint work, but in typical teenage banter I said, "Well it sure goes fast". We both stood admiring his pride and joy as he held a smile of satisfaction on his face. Suddenly there was a loud crack and a crash. The front wheel of the parked car just literally fell off and the front end crashed to the ground. "Oh! my! we've just been doing eighty miles per hour in that thing. We could have been killed," said I. He ran round to the front of the car, not really knowing much about cars. Not much knowledge about cars was needed as he pointed his hand at the front suspension and some rusted metal that had snapped. The car was on the scrap heap next day with my mate vowing to get revenge on the man who had sold him the car.

That very next day I was back at work at the office. I was a trainee accountant working for a prestigious firm of chartered accountants. Two of the bosses, known as "Partners", and both in late middle age, drove very nice cars indeed. One was an "E-Type" Jaguar. The other had a new top of the range Rover.

I realised all of a sudden that when we look at a car, we don't always see the person inside. A fast, new expensive car can be driven by a tired old man. An old, shabby small car can be driven by a younger man or woman at the height of their youthful looks and in their physical prime.

THE DOOR TO SPIRITUAL AWARENESS OPENED SLIGHLTLY. A realisation came over me that the real person inside each one of us is like the driver of a car. The thoughts came flooding in: A handsome or beautiful looking person might be uncaring, bad tempered, and self-centred. Another ordinary looking person could be totally caring and giving. When we die is it just as if we are a driver stepping out of our car? All the world ever saw was our physical body. The real "I" or "Me" inside is separate to our physical brain. Do we step out of ourselves at the end of physical life, look back and say: "Was that me?".

As these thoughts crossed my mind, I sensed something bigger at work. A spiritual "Someone" was helping me open the door to spiritual awareness.

The very first lesson in the road to sensing Angels is to actually accept that we are spiritual, and that another spiritual dimension or "Heaven" must exist. Opening this door to our beliefs is perhaps the most difficult because science tells us that we must find proof before we can accept anything as being real. How can we prove that we are of spirit? How can we convince our logical minds? After a lifetime of trying to find proof I realise that the spiritual world is another dimension. Scientific instruments are designed to take measurements in the physical dimension. It might be impossible for scientific instruments to measure the energies of another dimension.

So how can we ever prove anything spiritual? This can only be done by reaching logical conclusions from evidence that is totally convincing and withstands thorough investigation. The most convincing evidence is of course if we experience something supernatural ourselves.

THE BOOK OF LIFE

In our daily lives in the physical we are each day going through many experiences. Many of life's experiences are mundane, some are unpleasant, some are painful, hurtful, or experiences of fighting and hate. In contrast some experiences are happy, fun, or an experience that is an adventure. The most profoundly positive experience is that of love.

Each day we create a new page of the book of our life.

At some point in the future, when we have passed across to heaven, we can revisit those parts of our life we need to or want to. It is like turning to a certain page in a book. This is a book that we wrote, page by page, each day of our lives. We can jump into a video replay of that day that is so real that it is real to us. The days we choose to visit are those in which there were intense emotional experiences: either of happiness or sorrow, adventure and discovery or depression and despair; achievement, or loss.

When we go to a haunted house, often the haunting is the spirits of those who have lived in that house before. They are revisiting the place they want to visit, usually for some emotional reason. They are re-living different time periods and sometimes don't even notice you there in the present of today.

Hauntings

It is surprising how many people and families are troubled by ghosts and what seem to be evil spirits. Society around us doesn't accept such phenomena as real and so there is very little knowledge about what causes this phenomena and how to deal with it. If we learn to sense the Angels, tune in to Heaven, then we have an infinite amount of the most powerful energies of Heaven at our disposal to get rid of ghosts. We can command them to go with the full authority if Heaven.

I was called to a beautiful modern detached home. A normal respectable businessman and his wife had heard of me, and my ability to get rid of hauntings. Their three children, one young man, and two girls were in their early teens and very clued-up on being cool and fashionable. They seemed to view my visit with cool indifference. Their mum was certainly not cool. She was stressed and at the end of her wits. She immediately started to pour out an explanation of what was happening. Every night she would awake, pinned to her bed so tightly that she couldn't speak by some invisible force that she knew was an evil spirit. Her husband never witnessed this, but always slept through these incidents in a deep relaxed sleep. He had not experienced any weird experiences. She described lights flashing on and off and electrical appliances switching on and off, always when her husband was out. I spoke with the children who were not frightened but had heard footsteps on the stairs when no-one else was in the house, and all three had seen a ghost in the house, usually on the stairs. The ghost wasn't identifiable as male or female, but just a shadowy form.

Having listened to what they all had to say I firstly went to the stairway. There, hovering on the stairs was a grey mist. I knew this entity was the culprit, but what on earth was it? I then went down into the kitchen, directly beneath the stairs. I went alone. Confronting me was this grey mist, complete with a very scary head, menacing, and telling me to go. It was like a huge caterpillar, long, grey, hovering with this evil face in front of me. It was trying to scare me, but I was stronger. I knew this entity had been human at some time, but the person had been evil in life, and become so twisted in the afterlife as to completely lose its human identity. These things are depicted as fantasy in films that children watch. Our society is so misguided. These entities really exist and should not be taken lightly. I told the entity to go and leave this family alone. The entity became more frightening, came closer and gave a clear message that it was stopping where it was. For the first time I felt a shiver run up my spine. In the lounge I heard someone fall. A tough army friend of mine, a veteran of frontline fighting in Iraq, had been suddenly targeted by this spiritual energy, felt weird, very unwell, and collapsed. He had just come along out of genuine interest, but I feel also for his own amusement. He never expected this.

I had to think quickly and reverted back to my Christian Faith. I spoke out loudly with a prayer to God. "In the name of Jesus Christ, I command you to go." The entity retreated back. The solid walls of the house became transparent. I could still see this entity outside of the home, in the spiritual distance. "I pray to Father God to send the rescue Angels in to remove this entity." A beautiful Light appeared, and two Angels came out of the Light and grabbed the entity and took it away. My view of the scene became solid again, the walls of the house were now solid, and the entity gone. The atmosphere in the home had also, very suddenly, become normal, light, friendly, relaxed, and safe. I then asked my Angel Guide what had caused this evil entity to be in this house. I received a response immediately, now seeing clearly that the house was built on what is called a "Ley Line". These are lines of invisible energy criss-crossing the earth that were of great significance to ancient peoples because it is on these lines that Stonehenge, and other ancient monoliths were built. They are lines of intense spiritual energy. You know what? the ley line from their house also went straight through a hospital at the top of their road that at one time had been a sanatorium for people with mental illness. The time period of the sanatorium was around 100 years earlier. Quite a few lost souls were giving the residents of this new housing estate a scary time as I found out afterwards. I was subsequently called to clear several hauntings, both human and poltergeist, on this upmarket new housing estate. I feel sorry for others suffering such misery from evil spirits, or negative energy from misguided, lost souls. Many people suffer in silence, not knowing where to turn for help, and fearing that they will be ridiculed.

When I see children dressed like scary ghosts on Halloween, I don't find it child's play. I shudder and think "If only society, if only parents, knew the truth."

CHAPTER FIFTEEN

Do Animals Have a Soul?

nimals: Do they have a soul? The answer is YES! However, their conscious energy is not as big as ours. Imagine a large lake. An immense volume of water. Visualise this as being a sea of conscious energy. A bird, or a small mammal will have several drops, like raindrops, of conscious energy. A dog might have a cupful of conscious energy. We as human beings will each have a bucket full of conscious energy. In other words, our soul, the "I" or "Me" inside every one of us, is made up of conscious energy that is within all of life. Only we have more of it. Perhaps our inner soul is made up of the energies of many forms of life that have lived before. That is why, in our imagination, we can visualise ourselves being an animal. There is some part of us that will have experienced lives in bird and animal forms at a time in the distant past.

We can look at a dog or a cat and know there is someone looking back at us with a smaller conscious energy as a soul, but still capable of feeling emotions of happiness and sadness, and still in need of love. Never forget though that all animals function by the pre-programmed instincts of their brain which take control of their behaviour when they are in survival mode. All conscious energy is born out of God, and still linked to God which gives us the individual feeling of "One" or "Oneness" with life. We all have soulmates and seek to find some of our soulmates as we journey through life. Ultimately, we may merge with our soulmates, after this life, or a future life, to become a larger oneness of conscious energy that moves as one through new realms of experience.

Spiritual Research Into Animals Having a Soul

My research will no doubt be subject to criticism by scientists who study the workings of the brain. My conclusions are based on observing animal behaviour. The key identifier of soul consciousness is the ability to feel emotions. Higher level animals such as those classed as primates, dogs, cats, elephants, and others are seen to show emotions.

As an example, dogs can show excitement when playing or out for a walk or run. They can show sadness when missing someone or being left alone. They show anger and depression. Most importantly they can provide the highest emotion, that being love, towards their carer.

Of course, all animals have instinctive behaviour that is necessary for their survival. When they are in a hunting mode, or their instinctive reactions are triggered for other reasons, then their emotions are switched off.

This book is about Angels, and Angels do care for all animals. They bring in healing when needed. Often an Angel will work through the intuition of a human being to give that person feelings of a need to help the animal.

Angels take care of all of life in nature. I don't believe that insects have an individual spiritual consciousness within them, but the

Angels work hard to ensure that insect populations continue to do their part in maintaining the fragile balance of nature. Without this human beings would not exist.

CHAPTER SIXTEEN

Paranormal Energies

As we learn to sense Angels, we may also become more aware of other spiritual energies. These are mainly the Paranormal spiritual energies, which are widespread on the Earth Plain, and it is important to be able to identify them so that we can protect ourselves from any negative energies.

Good Souls who have passed across to Heaven

Such souls rarely manifest. They can be seen in clairvoyant visions of First Heaven, given by the Angels. Often a soul who has recently passed will need a time in First Heaven of adjusting to the soul state. I have been given many visions of souls being in a house or a garden similar to that of their Earthly home. It would seem that the quantum energies of a house on Earth are able to span the physical and spiritual dimensions to create a mirror -image of the house, garden, or any physical place in the spiritual dimension of First Heaven. Sometimes, if major work, such as a new kitchen or home extension are done to a physical house on Earth, it causes energy alterations to the mirror image replicated house in First Heaven. A soul in First Heaven might then manifest for a short period of time as a brief vision. In reality they are pushing their soul energies across to the Earth plain just to see what is going on! If we sense such energies it is nothing to be fearful of, but certainly very interesting!

Some people who lose a spouse, or a close family member, who lived in the same home instinctively feel that they need to change the decor and furniture straight away. This is because they feel spiritually ill at ease. Others feel that they want to keep everything as it was, perhaps feeling happier, sensing that the loved one who has passed still sits in the same chair or occupies the same room. This is possibly correct when we realise that there is a mirror-image replica of their home in First Heaven. Someone in First Heaven, sitting in a their favourite chair, can cause their spiritual energies to manifest in the chair in their physical home on Earth. This type of paranormal energy is not negative, and is harmless. As we learn to sense Angels, and become spiritually aware, it can help us recognise this phenomena happening in many places and many situations. I can look along a town centre street and see a replica street in First Heaven for every time period. Each time period is a layer with a different view. If I ask the Angels to give me a vision of say the year "1980" I am given visions of souls who still want to be on that street, but in First Heaven, reliving their memories of that year.

Ghosts

These are souls who have chosen not to pass across to Heaven. This is usually because they were evil in life and allowed their soul to become darkened with negative energy. Of course, souls cannot take their dark, negative energies across to Heaven. They will shed this soul energy if they do enter First Heaven, leaving them with a lot to account for in their Life Review.

It is an observation from my spiritual research that ghosts seem to cause distressing, frightening physical manifestations. As a person sensing Angels I know that we have the infinite power and strength of Heaven with us. We can command ghosts to "Go". We can further protect ourselves by making a prayer to God. I have cleared many hauntings from homes with the help of prayer and my Guardian Angel. Surprisingly ghostly happenings are not confined to old buildings. There are many hauntings experienced by ordinary families in modern homes.

Negative Entities

As previously explained, negative energy can darken the soul energy of a person. In time of battle during wars, many souls may die from their physical life. The anger that darkened their souls is shed before they enter Heaven and is left behind on the Earth plain, in the location where the battle occurred. Such negative energies can meld together to form a larger amount of negative energy that can manifest and be felt as a bad feeling, or even worse result in poltergeist or demonic activity on that area of land. Should housing eventually be built on that land, at a future date, manifestations can occur within the homes. For those who can sense and work with the Angels such negative energy can be removed, and we can protect ourselves from it. I have witnessed some very strange and frightening entities caused by this phenomena, but please be reassured that the help the Angels give is a strength far greater than such negative energies. I always succeed in removing them.

Negative Energies Influencing People

This is a widespread phenomena that has always caused humanity problems.

Self-centred people, lacking empathy for others, cause psycholigical and physical hurt. Their negative energy is generated from within their soul-being. However, for those who continually hurt others, exterior negative spiritual energies seize the opportunity to enter their soul and cause their behaviour towards others to become worse.

Hearing Voices in our mind

I have sometimes met with people who tell me that they hear voices in their mind. Obviously, the first thought is that they have some kind of mental illness. However, in some cases this is caused by negative spiritual energies. One such case was a man aged late twenties who had served in the armed forces, and two years later was discharged for health reasons. The first comment he made was to inform me that he was clairvoyant. I realised immediately that he was much too open to any spiritual energies. He could see across to the Spiritual Realm, but was also open to negative earthbound energies. He told me about voices in his head that would tell him to do things which hurt him. These negative influences were so compelling that he would do many dangerous things that resulted in injury to himself. On one occasion negative entities told him to run barefoot for twelve miles on a gravel road and then jump into a rapid flowing river, which he did. Fortunately, he wasn't injured and the cold river water gave him a shock that pulled him out of the negative influence.

Negative earthbound energies try to steer the behaviour of people into hurting others, or hurting animals and nature. If negative energy cannot provoke behaviour that hurts others, it will influence the behaviour of the person to self-harm. I believe that many cases of self-harm have a spiritual cause. The victim of self-harm might go through a period where they feel a void, a darkness inside, that tells them to self-harm. This might be followed by a period of normality where they are more resistant to these negative influences.

Case Study

A lady, Janet (not her real name), aged mid-twenties attended a meeting where I was giving group readings of Angel messages. When it came to her turn for a reading I was immediately given a vision of her being physically and mentally hurt and abused by her male partner. She constantly sought to protect her four year old daughter. I told her this and she confirmed that as correct. I then gave her some messages via the Angels from her grandma in spirit. In group readings, which I give freely without charge, I can only give a few minutes to each person. Around a month later she again came to my group meeting. Her situation was still the same, if not worse. She looked pale and was genuinely frightened to leave her partner. I could see that negative energies had been generated within her partner and that he had drawn in more negative energies to turn him into a very cruel and controlling man. She had to leave him, but I never give advice concerning relationships.

My thoughts were "This is time to speak to her about her Guardian Angel". I was told by the Angels that they had tried to warn her not to enter into a relationship with this man. I discussed this with her, and she admitted that her inner feelings had given her warnings, but she had seen his aggressive attitude to the world as a sign of the strength she had been looking for in a man. As often happens, he had been well behaved towards her in the earlier months of their relationship, living together. His aggressive behaviour towards her started at the birth of their daughter. I could only spare Janet a few minutes but I explained how our Guardian Angels are real. As with many people, she had become convinced of this through the accuracy of the Angels readings I had given her. I said: "Listen to yout intuition. That is how your Guardian Angel will speak to you. Listen every step of the way. You will be guided to a safer, happier furure".

About three months later Janet came to my meeting again. She looked healthy and happy. She told that she had listened to the intuitive messages and guidance from her Guardian Angel. She had made careful plans to find secretly find another home for herself and her daughter, and made the move suddenly one day when her partner was out (he didn't have employment). He had since made threats against her, so her life was still very stressful, but she felt she could now plan her future with greater confidence. One year later she came to see me again. With the help of the intuitive messages from her Guardian Angel she was now working again as a self-employed hairdresser. Her mother wasn't afraid to call to see her in her new home and was helping with child care. She said "Do you see a new partner in my life?" I was immediately given a vision of a man. I described him in detail, including the colour of his hair, his eyes, the clothes he liked to wear, and the work that he does. She gasped in astonishment and took a photo from her bag of a man. She said: "Is this him?" The photo was identical to the man whom I had just described. "He is my new boyfriend, but I am reluctant to open my feelings up to him". I said: "The Angels have brought you both together. Perhaps you can trust him. Keep moving through life listening to your intuitive feelings". She laughed and said: "I will".

Our Guardian Angels
Having described negative energies, it is important to remind ourselves that we can learn to connect only with the unconditional love of Heaven and our Guardian Angels. Being able to identify negative energies means we can avoid their influence and tell them to go away. We can make a prayer to God and be confident of the absolute protection of the Guardian Angels from Heaven.

CONCLUSION

The Afterlife of Heaven is real, and the Angels in Heaven are working constantly in genuine love and care for humanity, for nature and for planet Earth.

There are over seven billion people alive on this planet and the future of all of us is as complex as each of the individual futures of the seven billion.

I urge the world to try to believe that we are truly spiritual children of God and that we can learn to recognise and act on our individual callings to do some good in this world. Together we can save planet Earth from the worst consequences of climate change. Heaven is real and Angels are real. Individually we can learn to sense our Guardian Angels so that we can be guided by them to stay safe, and work towards a happier and fulfilling future. Sensing the Angels can truly bring miracles into our lives.